Lonely planet

POCKET

DUBAI

TOP EXPERIENCES • LOCAL LIFE

T0017999

ANDREA SCHULTE-PEEVERS,
JOSEPHINE QUINTERO

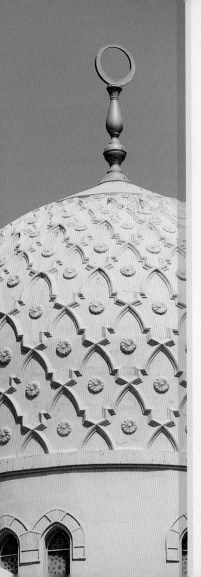

Contents

Plan Your Trip 4

Jumeirah Mosque (p74)
STEVE LOVEGROVE/SHUTTERSTOCK ©

COVID-19

We have re-checked every business in this book before publication to ensure that it is still open after the COVID-19 outbreak. However, the economic and social impacts of COVID-19 will continue to be felt long after the outbreak has been contained, and many businesses, services and events referenced in this guide may experience ongoing restrictions. Some businesses may be temporarily closed, have changed their opening hours and services, or require bookings; some will unfortunately have closed their doors permanently. We suggest you check with venues before visiting for the latest information.

Top Experiences

Enjoy the views from Burj Khalifa (p102)

UMAR SHARIF/SHUTTERSTOCK © ARCHITECT: ADRIAN SMITH

Wander through Al Fahidi Historic District (p52)

Look and learn at Dubai Museum (p50)

Sip cocktails at Burj Al Arab (p88)

Wander the Gold Souq's wooden arcades (p32)

S-F/SHUTTERSTOCK ©

Shop, eat and play at Dubai Mall (p104)

Step into a modern souq at Madinat Jumeirah (p86)

R.A.R. DE BRUIJN HOLDING BV/SHUTTERSTOCK ©

Explore art and culture in Abu Dhabi (p142)

Marvel at the Museum of the Future (p106)

WALTER BIBIKOW/SHUTTERSTOCK ©

VINNIKAVA VIKTORYIA/SHUTTERSTOCK © ARCHITECT: SHAUN KILLA

Dining Out

Dining in Dubai is an extraordinarily multicultural experience. Arabic and Indian fare are the most prevalent, but you can feast on anything from kebabs to fish and chips in the city's myriad eateries. These run the gamut from simple street kitchens to luxe dining temples.

Farm to Fork

Taking global fare local is not unique to Dubai, but it's arrived with a vengeance. As awareness has grown, demand for certified organic produce has increased right along with it. Farms in the UAE have expanded their operations, and farmers markets pop up all over. Even supermarkets have joined the locavore trend by marking the origin of their produce.

Emirati Cuisine

Restaurants serving Emirati food (pictured) used to be rare, but thankfully this is changing. Typical dishes are one-pot stews featuring a combination of grains, vegetables and meat or fish, flavoured with spices and topped with nuts or dried fruit.

Camel Milk

Known to Bedouin for centuries, the health benefits of camel milk have caught international attention. Slightly pungent and salty in taste, it's lower in fat and more vitamin-rich than cow's milk. Restaurants have also started to put camel dishes on their menus, although it's not traditionally an Emirati staple.

Best Cheap Eats

Ravi Empty tables are as rare as hen's teeth at this unfussy curry temple with sidewalk seating. (p77)

Al Ustad Special Kabab All manner of people fill this cool been-here-forever Iranian kebab joint. (p62)

Al Tawasol Sit on the floor Bedouin-style for a cutlery-free classic Yemeni feast. (p42)

11

Plan Your Trip Dining Out

ZURIJETA/SHUTTERSTOCK ©

Best Emirati Food

Logma Casual cafe that serves modern Emirati cuisine from breakfast to dessert. (p77)

Aseelah Successfully bridges traditional and contemporary Emirati food and decor. (p42)

Al Fanar This traditional spot is an ode to Emirati culinary heritage. (p78)

Best Middle Eastern

Qwaider Al Nabulsi Makes fluffy falafel and some of the best *kunafa* (vermicelli-like pastry soaked in syrup) in town. (p42)

Zaroob Lebanese street-food staples in an urban indoor setting. (p113)

Best Indian

Indego by Vineet Michelin man Vineet Bhatia seduces diners with contemporary spins on Indian classics. (p134)

Eric's Unassuming neighbourhood charmer delivers a taste-bud tingling culinary journey to Goa. (p63)

Sind Punjab Spicy budget curries are the currency at one of Dubai's oldest Indian eateries. (p62)

Best Vegetarian

Saravana Bhavan Don't let the unassuming decor put you off – the all-veg Indian food is tops. (p63)

Govinda's Serves Sattvic food that not only eschews meat but also oil, onion and garlic. (p64)

Top Tips for Dining Out

Make weekend bookings, including Saturday brunch, for top tables at least a week ahead. Note that only licensed hotel restaurants and independent venues may serve alcohol.

Bar Open

Dubai may be famous for glam clubs, but it's also developing a more low-key underground scene. Dubai's weekend nights are busiest, when party animals let off steam in bars and on the dance floor. Alcohol is served in hotels and some licensed venues only.

Bars & Pubs

Venues in Downtown Dubai, Jumeirah, Dubai Marina and Palm Jumeirah tend to appeal mostly to well-heeled visitors and expats. Beachfront lounges and rooftop bars continue to be popular. Bars and pubs in Bur Dubai and Deira are more low-key, gritty affairs. Note that prostitution, though officially illegal, is tolerated in many establishments.

Shisha & Mocktails

Most Emiratis don't drink alcohol, preferring to socialise over coffee, juice and mocktails. Join them in a mellow shisha cafe and sample a puff to better understand this Middle Eastern pastime.

Happy Hours & Ladies' Nights

Take advantage of happy hours offered by most bars, from dives to five-star lounges. Many go to great lengths to lure women with free cocktails, bubbly and nibbles, especially on Tuesdays and Wednesdays.

Best Beachfront Bars

Jetty Lounge Sip artful potions while tucked into an overstuffed sofa at this sensuously styled bar. (p138)

Bliss Lounge Chilled Dubai Marina dispensary of some of the finest cocktails in town. (p138)

Zero Gravity Bustling beach club with restaurant and bar. (p136)

Best Rooftop Bars

Siddharta Lounge Cocktails with a view of the glittering Dubai Marina at this ab-fab lounge by the pool. (p138)

40 Kong Power players loosen their ties and inhibitions at this swank outdoor bar. (p118)

HEMIS/ALAMY ©

Treehouse Cocktails with views of Burj Khalifa in posh living-room-style cosiness. (p117)

Best for Happy Hours & Ladies' Nights

Pure Sky Lounge Sunsets over the Gulf go well with half-price drinks daily between 5pm and 7pm. (p138)

Bahri Bar Three free glasses of bubbly in this Arabian-styled bar with Burj Al Arab views. (p97)

Lucky Voice Buy one, get one free every day from 4pm to 8pm. (p137)

Barasti Beachfront institution; 30% drink discounts daily, plus bottomless

sparkly for women on Tuesdays. (p137)

Best Pubs

Irish Village The classic is still going strong after nearly 20 years in business. (p44)

Fibber Magee's A bit down at the heel, but that just adds to the character of this perennial pub fave. (p118)

George & Dragon Channel your inner Bukowski at this hardcore barfly hangout. (p66)

Best for Shisha & Mocktails

QDs Puff away languidly while looking out on the shimmering Creek and skyline. (pictured; p45)

Top Tips for a Night Out

Dubai has zero-tolerance laws on drink driving. Getting caught could entail fines or jail time. Note, too, that since 2016, Dubai bars are also open – and serve alcohol – during Ramadan. Most clubs close during this period.

Treasure Hunt

Shopping is a favourite pastime in Dubai, which boasts not only the world's largest mall but also shopping centres that resemble ancient Egypt or an Italian village and feature ski slopes, ice rinks and giant aquariums. Souqs provide more traditional flair, and a growing crop of urban outdoor malls, indie boutiques and galleries beckon as well.

Trends

Recently, urban outdoor malls have arrived, those such as BoxPark in Jumeirah and City Walk near Downtown Dubai, with a smaller selection of stores calibrated to the needs and tastes of neighbourhood residents. There's also a growing crop of indie designer boutiques as well as thriving flea markets.

Bargaining Basics

Prices in malls and most stores are fixed, but in souqs and outdoor markets it pays to know some bargaining basics. A good rule of thumb is to cut the first suggested price in half and go from there. Expect to finish up with a discount of 20% to 30%. For more tips, see A Primer on Bargaining (p47).

Carpet Buying

Dubai has a reputation in the region for having the highest-quality carpets at the best prices. Fine Persian carpets, colourful Turkish and Kurdish kilims and rough-knotted Bedouin rugs are all widely available. Bargaining is the norm. If buying, be sure to ask for a Certificate of Authentication issued by the Dubai Chamber of Commerce & Industry.

Best Shopping Malls

Dubai Mall A power shopper's Shangri-La, Dubai Mall is the largest shopping mall in the world. (p104)

Mall of the Emirates Get lost amid the ample temptations of this mega-mall famous for its indoor ski slope. (pictured; p99)

BoxPark This urban strip brims with cool cafes and eclectic boutiques in shipping containers. (p81)

S-F/SHUTTERSTOCK ©

Best Markets

Ripe Market Happening market in Zabeel Park with quality local produce, handmade art and craft and international food stalls. (p68)

Dubai Flea Market Bargains abound at this monthly market on the beautiful grounds of Zabeel Park. (p67)

Best for Indie Fashion

S*uce Home-grown concept store showcases regional designers in fashion, accessories and jewellery. (p82)

O Concept This edgy Jumeirah boutique has young things looking good at reasonable prices. (p82)

Best Modern Souqs

Souk Al Bahar Across from Dubai Mall, this richly decorated Arabesque souq teems with restaurants and souvenir stores. (p120)

Souk Madinat Jumeirah This tourist-geared souq follows a harmonious rhythm of courtyards, alleyways and outdoor areas. (p87)

Best for Gifts & Souvenirs

Bateel Delicious dates presented like precious jewels in an elegant boutique setting. (p68)

Mirzam Dubai's own chocolate factory wraps its yummy single-origin bean bars in artistic designs. (p91)

Deira Fish Market

Deira's **fish market** (📞800 627 538; www.waterfrontmarket.ae; Al Khaleej Rd, Waterfront Market, near Abu Hail St; 🕐10am-10pm Sun-Wed, to 11pm Thu & Fri; 🚌17, C15, Ⓜ Abu Hail, Gold Souq) is full of bustle and bargains. Wriggling lobsters, shrimp the size of small bananas, metre-long kingfish and mountains of blue crab are a photogenic feast.

For Kids

Travelling to Dubai with kids can be child's play. There's plenty to do – from water parks and playgrounds to theme parks and activity centres. Most beach resorts operate kids' clubs, giving you ample peace to work on your tan or skip off to the spa.

Junior Foodies

Kids are welcome at all but the most formal restaurants, although you might feel more relaxed at casual spots. All malls boast extensive food courts, and hotels have at least one restaurant suitable for families. There's also a growing crop of kid-geared cafes.

Playgrounds & Parks

Dubai has a handful of parks with picnic areas and playgrounds for children to let off steam (just don't go in the searing heat of July and August). One of the biggest and best for activities is Zabeel Park (p60), home of the Dubai Frame (p59).

Teen Time

OK, so they've done the ski slopes, disco-danced at the ice rink, splashed around at the water parks and enjoyed a fashionable strut around the malls. Is there more to prevent teens from succumbing to boredom? To impress their pals back home, consider taking them sandboarding, camel riding on an overnight desert safari or even a trekking trip to the Hajar Mountains.

Best Water Parks

Aquaventure Waterpark
One of the largest water parks in the world with lots of rides for thrill junkies. (pictured; p129)

Wild Wadi Waterpark Family favourite with attractions ranging from gentle pools to kamikaze slides. (p95)

KOTSOVOLOS PANAGIOTIS/SHUTTERSTOCK ©

Best for Animal Attractions

Dubai Aquarium & Underwater Zoo Kids will be mesmerised by the sharks, groupers and rays flitting about this giant three-storey aquarium in Dubai Mall. (p105)

Lost Chambers Aquarium For another audience with fishy friends, head to this labyrinth of underwater tanks and tunnels teeming with exotic denizens at Atlantis The Palm. (p129)

Green Planet This indoor rainforest brings the tropics to the desert, complete with birds, frogs, lizards, butterflies, turtles and other critters. (p75)

Best for Chilled-out Kids

Dubai Ice Rink Tots to teens can cool down with pirouettes and disco dancing at Dubai Mall's ice rink. (p111)

Ski Dubai Alpine slopes, toboggan tracks and penguin encounters await at this massive indoor winter wonderland. (p95)

Top Tips for Travelling with Children

Many hotels have kids clubs and child-care centres. For babysitting, ask for a referral at your hotel or try www.dubaimetromaids.com or www.maidszone.com. Note, too, in Dubai, children under five travel free on public transport.

Clubbing

DJs spin every night of the week with the top names hitting the decks on Fridays and Saturdays. Partying is not restricted to nighttime; plenty of beach clubs open at midday on weekends in the cooler months.

AZIMORUNOV/SHUTTERSTOCK ©

Global DJs

Globetrotting big-name DJs like Ellen Allien and Steve Aoki occasionally jet in for the weekend to whip the crowd into a frenzy in the top venues and at mega-parties like Groove on the Grass or Party in the Park. But there's plenty of resident spin talent as well.

Best for Top DJs

White Dubai Megaclub with dizzying light show on top of the Meydan Racecourse. (p119)

Base State-of-the-art partying in this giant club in Dubai Design District. (p118)

Best for Outdoor Partying

Barasti Any time is a good time to stumble into the original party village in the sand. (p137)

Zero Gravity Bustling beach club with restaurant and bar. (p136)

White Dubai Beiruti import is a glitterati fave. (p119)

Best Vibes

Club Boudoir Swish venue for beautiful people gyrating to a sound mix from hip-hop to desi (Bollywood). (p80)

Cavalli Club Bling briga-diers should strap on those heels and make a beeline for this sparkling dancing den. (p118)

Top Tips for Clubbing

Keep tabs on club news with the free biweekly *Hype* magazine, available at bars, boutiques, gyms and spas. Other listings include www.dubainight.com, www.residentadvisor.net and www.timeout.com

Under the Radar

It may be tough to resist the siren call of Dubai's star attractions, but beyond the crowd(ed) favourites awaits an entire galaxy of fun experiences sure to surprise and enlighten you. Simply venture beyond the glamour and connect with local life in low-key neighbourhoods and pristine nature spots.

ALEXEYS/GETTY IMAGES ©

Desert Escapes

Even just a day spent listening to the secrets of the sands will add a more sensory dimension to your UAE adventure. For encounters with roaming gazelles, oryx and camels, head to the **Dubai Desert Conservation Reserve** (www.ddcr.org; **P**; pictured) on your own or with a tour operator. If you want the full desert immersion, treat yourself to an overnight stay at the superluxe **Al Maha Desert Resort & Spa** (📞04 832 9900; www.al-maha.com;

Dubai Desert Conservation Reserve, Dubai–Al Ain Rd (Hwy E66); full board from Dhs6100; **P** 🛜 ⌘). Action-oriented types should attend a camel race at **Al Marmoom Race Track** (📞04 832 6526; www.dcrc.ae; off Dubai–Al Ain Rd (Hwy E66); ⌚Nov-Apr).

Best for Shopping

Karama Market Join locals in the hunt for bargains at this old-school shopping strip (p69), then feast on fragrant Goan fare at **Eric's**. (p63)

Waterfront Market Pick your fave finny feast at this vast 24/7 fish market, then

have it cut, cleaned and cooked up at an on-site restaurant. (p15)

Best Museums

Jameel Arts Center (www.jameelartscentre.org) Contemporary art space overlooking Dubai Creek.

Women's Museum Shines the spotlight on the accomplishments of Emirati women. (p39)

Best Public Art

La Mer Bustling beachfront village bristling with Insta-suited murals. (p79)

Dubai Design District Street art, sculptures and installations in an edgy style hub on Dubai Canal. (p110)

Art

GIUSEPPE CACACE/GETTYIMAGES ©

Fueled by artists from around the world, Dubai's art scene has become one of the most dynamic in the Gulf region. Art aficionados will find their compass on perpetual spin with a growing number of galleries, private collections, street art and high-profile art events.

Gallery Quarters

Galleries in Dubai cluster in two main areas: emerging, underground and experimental art in the Alserkal Avenue campus (pictured) in industrial Al Quoz, and more established contenders in Gate Village. Dubai art-world pioneers cluster around Bur Dubai's Al Fahidi Historic District.

Urban & Street Art

Dubai's urban art scene has developed thanks to the Dubai Street Museum project. Large-scale murals celebrating the UAE's history decorate 2nd December St in Satwa, and funky creations line City Walk in Jumeirah. Artful graffiti is also scattered around the Al Fahidi Historic District in Bur Dubai.

Dubai Art Week

Held annually in March, Dubai Art Week centres on Art Dubai (www.artdubai. ae), a gathering of nearly 100 galleries from the UAE and abroad at Madinat Jumeirah. There's also Design Days Dubai and the Sikka Art and Design Festival (www. sikkartandesign.com), for which local artists create site-specific works in the Al Fahidi Historic District.

Best for Middle Eastern Art

Ayyam Gallery This top international gallery has branches in both Alserkal Avenue and Gate Village. (p110)

Third Line Represents top regional artists here and at international art fairs. (p91)

Leila Heller Gallery Art-world top dogs and promising up-and-comers. (p91)

Gallery Isabelle van den Eynde Shepherds regional emerging and midcareer artists to prominence. (p91)

Tours

FRANTIC00/GETTY IMAGES ©

If you're a Dubai first-timer, letting someone else show you around is a fun and efficient way to get your bearings, see the key sights quickly and obtain a general understanding of the city. All manner of exploration – from city bus tours to mosque visits – is available.

Dubai in Depth

Dubai offers a growing number of guided explorations to match all sorts of interests. Take a classic bus tour if you just want to get an introduction to the city or join a themed walking tour for an in-depth look at certain facets of daily life. Based in Bur Dubai, the nonprofit Sheikh Mohammed Centre for Cultural Understanding offers the best cultural tours to introduce visitors to facets of Emirati culture, including traditions, customs and religion. They're the only ones who take non-Muslims inside a mosque and also offer meals where you can taste the local cuisine.

Best Walking Tours

Al Fahidi Historic District Peel back the curtain on Dubai's distant past on a tour with the Sheikh Mohammed Centre for Cultural Understanding. (p58)

Frying Pan Adventures Plunge headlong into the culinary labyrinth of multicultural Bur Dubai and Deira on these fun and educational guided food tours. (p64)

Jumeirah Mosque The only mosque in Dubai that can be visited by non-Muslims; guided tours offered daily except Friday. (p74)

Best Bus Tours

Big Bus Dubai Hop-on, hop-off tours with taped commentary in 12 languages link all of Dubai's major sights and landmarks on three interconnecting routes. (pictured; p61)

Wonder Bus Tours Discover Dubai's historic centre on one-hour land and water tours aboard an ingenious amphibious bus. (p76)

Best Boat Tours

Dubai Ferry Value-priced minicruises let you appreciate the city skyline from the water. (p66)

Al Mansour Dhow Float past the glittering Creek lights while indulging in a buffet dinner on a historic dhow. (p43)

Four Perfect Days

Day 1

ZELJKODAN/SHUTTERSTOCK ©

Follow our **Bur Dubai Waterside Walk** (p54) through the **Al Fahidi** (p52) and **Shindagha** (p59) historic districts. Hop on the ferry to Deira to peruse the dazzling **Spice** (pictured; p38), **Gold** (p32) and **Perfume** (p38) souqs, then board the metro at Gold Souq station.

Glimpse life in 2070 at the **Museum of the Future** (p106), then jolt back to the present at **Dubai Mall** (p104), with 1200 stores plus an **aquarium** (p105) and an **ice rink** (p111). It's dwarfed by the sky-piercing **Burj Khalifa** (p102).

Coming down, admire the **Dubai Fountain** (p105), take a taxi to Madinat Jumeirah for dinner with Burj Al Arab views at **Pierchic** (p96), then finish with quiet drinks at **Bahri Bar** (p97).

Day 2

ASHRAF HAMDAN/SHUTTERSTOCK ©

Join the guided tour of the gorgeous **Jumeirah Mosque** (p74), a rare one in Dubai open to non-Muslims, then walk over to the **Etihad Museum** (p74) to learn about the founding of the UAE.

Try a traditional Emirati lunch at **Al Fanar** (p78), then relax on the sands for a couple of hours on **Kite** (pictured; p94) or **JBR** (p130) beach.

Rinse off the salt for happy hour cocktails at **Bliss Lounge** (p138) or **Pure Sky Lounge** (p138). For dinner, decide between views of the Gulf at **Indego by Vineet** (p134) or the yachts in the marina at **Asia Asia** (p134). Wind down the night in style on the breezy terrace of **Siddharta Lounge** (p138).

Day 3

FOKKE BAARSSEN/SHUTTERSTOCK ©

Kickstart the day with coffee at hip **Nightjar Coffee** (p113), followed by a gallery hop around the **Alserkal Avenue** (p90) warehouse complex.

Get a taxi to the **Mall of the Emirates** (p99) to see **Ski Dubai** (pictured; p95) and spend the early afternoon keeping cool here or getting wet at the **Wild Wadi Waterpark** (p95). Go for Insta-gold at **The View at the Palm** (p130), then grab a sunset cocktail on **Palm West Beach** (p131) before wrapping up at **101 Lounge & Bar** (p134) by marveling at the twinkling skyscrapers while you dine. Grab the restaurant's free shuttle back to the mainland.

Day 4

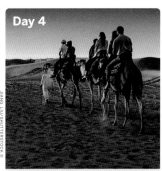

JIANG_LIU/SHUTTERSTOCK ©

It's time to sample desert serenity on the authentic Bedouin Culture Safari with **Platinum Heritage Tours** (p132). It includes a camel ride to a desert camp where you join Bedu for breakfast and meet their hunting dogs and falcons. You'll be back in town around noon.

Aquaventure Waterpark (p129) is guaranteed to give you a thrill. It's filled with fun and exciting slides and plunges, and an afternoon spent here passes in no time.

For dinner, head to The Walk at JBR for scrumptious Italian fare at **BiCE** (p137), then finish with a stroll along **The Beach at JBR** (p128).

Need to Know

For detailed information, see Survival Guide (p145)

Currency
Dirham (Dhs)

Languages
Arabic, English, Urdu

Visas
Citizens of over 50 countries are eligible for free entry visas valid for either 30 days (eg UK, USA, Australia, Ireland) or 90 days (all EU countries except Ireland) on arrival in Dubai.

Money
ATMs are widely available. Credit cards are accepted in most hotels, restaurants and shops.

Mobile Phones
Mobile phones operate on GSM900/1800. Local SIM cards are easy to find in electronics stores and some grocery stores.

Time
Gulf Standard Time (GMT/UTC plus four hours)

Daily Budget

Budget: Less than Dhs600
Budget hotel room: Dhs300–400
Meal in a food court: Dhs20–50
Public transport: Dhs1–8.50

Midrange: Dhs600–1200
Double room in a hotel: Dhs400–700
Two-course meal without alcohol in a restaurant: from Dhs80
Entry to top attractions and sights: Dhs100–200

Top end: More than Dhs1200
Four-star hotel room: from Dhs800
Three-course fine-dining meal with wine: from Dhs400
Drinks in a high-end bar: from Dhs100

Advance Planning

Three months or more before Double-check visa regulations. Book tickets for high-profile sporting and entertainment events.

One month before Reserve a table at top restaurants and tickets for Burj Khalifa. Check concert venue websites for what's on during your stay.

One week before Check average daytime temperatures and pack accordingly.

Arriving in Dubai

Taxis and the Dubai metro are both convenient modes of transport to/from the airport. Note that cabbies navigate not by addresses but by landmarks (such as malls, big hotels, beaches).

✈ Dubai International Airport

Metro Red Line runs every few minutes between 6am and midnight, from terminals 1 and 3.
Bus Buses take over from Metro from midnight to 6am.
Taxis Flag fall of Dhs25; Dhs50 to Deira, Dhs80 to Downtown Dubai.

✈ From Al Maktoum International Airport

Bus F55 goes to Ibn Battuta metro station to connect to Dubai Metro Red Line.
Taxis Around Dhs70 to Dubai Marina and Dhs110 to Downtown Dubai.

Getting Around

The Dubai metro is an inexpensive, speedy and comfortable mode of transport. Buses offer good coverage but are slow and have baffling timetables. Before using public transport, you must purchase a rechargeable pass (Nol card; www.nol.ae) from ticket offices or vending machines.

🚇 Metro

Red and Green Lines link all major sights and neighbourhoods, and run from 5am to 1.15am Monday to Thursday (to 2.15am Friday and Saturday) and from 8am until 1.15am on Sunday.

🚕 Taxi

Taxis are metered, air-conditioned and the fastest and most comfortable way to get around, except during rush hour. Hail in the street, at taxi ranks or book by phone and the free Smart Taxi App.

🚗 Uber & Careem

Ride-hailing apps such as Uber (www.uber.com) and Dubai-based Careem (www.careem.com).

🚌 Bus

Fairly slow, but clean and useful for stops not served by the metro.

⛴ Boat

Abras (traditional wooden ferries) cross the Creek between Deira and Bur Dubai. The Dubai Ferry operates on two interlinking routes along the Dubai Canal and between Bur Dubai and Dubai Marina.

🚊 Tram

The Dubai Tram travels along King Salman Bin Abdulaziz Al Saud St between Dubai Media City and Dubai Marina.

Dubai Neighbourhoods

Dubai Marina & Palm Jumeirah (p123)
Tailor-made for hedonists, this area entices with beaches, luxury hotels, a pedestrian-friendly marina and sizzling nightlife.

Burj Al Arab

Madinat Jumeirah

Burj Al Arab & Madinat Jumeirah (p85)
A modern Arabian village with superb beaches, restaurants and souvenir shopping, backed by the iconic Burj Al Arab.

Downtown Dubai (p101)
The Burj Khalifa presides over the city's futuristic centre with plenty to delight shoppers, families and art and architecture fans alike.

Jumeirah & Around (p71)
Hugging a fabulous stretch of beach, this villa-studded residental area also has plenty in store for fashionistas and adventurous foodies.

Bur Dubai (p49)
Dubai's historic hub is a polycultural potpourri of restored buildings, budget eateries, shopping bargains and photogenic Creek views.

Dubai Museum ◉ ◉ Gold Souq
◉
Al Fahidi Historic District

Burj Khalifa ◉
◉ Museum of the Future
◉
Dubai Mall

✈ Dubai International Airport

Deira (p31)
Charismatic, crowded and cacophonous, Deira's twisting roads are loaded with atmospheric souqs, heritage sites and fantastic eats.

Explore
Dubai

Explore ✧

Deira

Hugging the northern side of the Creek, Deira is one of Dubai's oldest and most charismatic neighbourhoods. Dusty, crowded and chaotic, it feels a world away from the skyscraper-studded modern districts along Sheikh Zayed Rd. Along the Creek, colourful wooden dhows plough their time-tested trade between Iran, Sudan and other locales. Nearby, the bustling souqs are ancestors to today's malls, where you can sip tea and haggle for bargains with traders tending generations-old stores.

The most historic area is Al Ras, near the mouth of the Creek, home to century-old pearl traders' homes and the city's first school, but Deira's most seductive lure is its cluster of atmospheric souqs. This tangle of narrow lanes heaves with a cacophony of sounds and smells that bursts to life in the morning and late afternoon.

Deira is also Dubai's most dazzlingly multicultural neighbourhood, peacefully shared by immigrants from around the globe. Many operate restaurants perfect for sampling classic fare from places such as India, Syria, Lebanon, Ethiopia, Iraq and Afghanistan. Alternatively, book a dinner cruise aboard a festively decorated dhow, or head to a Creekside alfresco lounge in a high-end hotel.

Getting There & Around

The main sights of Deira are all within easy walking distance of each other around the mouth of Dubai Creek.

Deira is served by the metro's Red and Green Lines, which intersect at Union station. The Red Line travels to the airport. Abras link the souqs in Deira and Bur Dubai across the Creek.

Neighbourhood Map on p36

Shoes for sale, Deira ANASTASIOS71/SHUTTERSTOCK ©

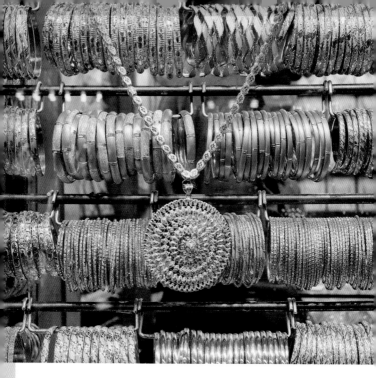

Top Experience 📷

Wander the Gold Souq's Wooden Arcades

'Dubai: City of Gold' screams the banner atop the LED display at the towering entrance gate to Dubai's Gold Souq; you'll feel as though you've just plunged into a latter-day Aladdin's cave. Lining a wooden-latticed central arcade and spidery lanes are hundreds of shops spilling over with gold, diamonds, pearls, silver and platinum. It's a dazzling display and a must-see.

⊙ MAP P36, B2

Sikkat Al Khail St

🕙 10am-1pm & 3-10pm

Ⓜ Al Ras

The Real Deal?

No need to worry about fakes at the Gold Souq. The quality of gold is government-regulated, so you can be fairly confident that the piece of jewellery you've got your eye on is genuine (unlike the Rolex watches or Prada bags touts are trying to tempt you with). Price is determined by weight based on the official daily international rate and on the artistry of the item. Haggling is expected and vendors build in price buffers accordingly. Sharp bargaining skills usually make merchants drop the initial asking price by 20% to 30%. The price of gold itself is fixed, so focus on the intricacy of the artisanship as a point of discussion.

Record-Breaking Gold Ring

Dubai being the capital of superlatives, the Gold Souq is naturally home to a record-breaking piece of jewellery. Stop at the Kanz shop just past the main souq entrance (off Old Baladiya St) to snap a selfie with the world's largest and heaviest gold ring, as certified by none other than Guinness World Records. Called the Najmat Taiba (Star of Taiba), the 21-carat beauty weighs in at nearly 64kg and is worth a hefty US$3 million.

People-Watching

Simply watching the goings-on at the souq is another treat, especially during the bustling evenings. Settle down on a bench, buy a bottle of juice from one of the itinerant sellers and take in the colourful street theatre. With a little patience, you should see hard-working Afghan men dragging heavy carts of goods, African women in bright kaftans balancing their purchases on their heads, and chattering local women out on a shopping spree.

★ **Top Tips**

o The best time to visit is in the bustling evenings; mornings are busy with tour groups and afternoons sleepy.

o Credit cards are almost always accepted, but you'll get a better price with cash.

o If you don't see anything you like, don't panic. Most shops will make something to your own design.

o Don't rush! Remember, you don't have to make a decision on the spot. Compare carefully before you buy and be prepared to haggle.

✕ **Take a Break**

A classic pit stop in these parts is **Ashwaq** (☎04 226 1164; cnr Al Soor & Sikkat Al Khail Sts; sandwiches Dhs4-7; ⊙8.30am-midnight; M Gold Souq), whose shawarma rocks the palate. Wash it down with a freshly squeezed fruit juice.

Deira Wander the Gold Souq's Wooden Arcades

Walking Tour 🥾

Deira Souq Stroll

The Deira souq area is one of the most historic and atmospheric districts in Dubai and is best explored by foot. It's a bustling, nicely chaotic warren of lanes teeming with exotic stalls and shops and especially bustling in the evenings. This tour covers the main bazaars and also incorporates a couple of heritage stops into its route.

Walk Facts

Start Deira Old Souq abra station

End Afghan Khorasan Kebab

Length 2km; three hours

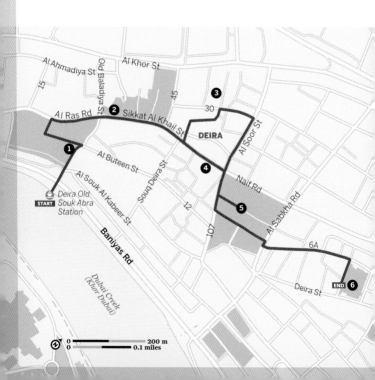

❶ Spice Souq

As soon as you step off the abra at Deira Old Souq abra station, heady scents will lure you across to the **Spice Souq** (p38). Follow your nose around to find saffron, turmeric, frankincense and more. To learn about one of Dubai's finest poets, pop into the **Museum of the Poet Al Oqaili** (p39)

❷ Gold Souq

Find your way to Al Ras Rd and turn right to Old Baladiya St. Find the wooden latticed entrance gate of the **Gold Souq** (p32), easily recognised by the lettering 'City of Gold'. Take a selfie with the world's largest gold ring, then peruse the bling, from petite earrings to over-the-top gold pieces created for bridal dowries.

❸ Women's Museum

Head north of the central arcade to suss out tiny teashops, cafeterias, busy tailors and barber shops in narrow lanes. Look for signs to the **Women's Museum** (p39) to learn about contributions made by Emirati women in such fields as art, science and education.

❹ Perfume Souq

Head back south and turn left onto 32a St, then follow it to Al Soor St and the **Perfume Souq** (p38). Turn right and sniff out pungent Arabian *attars* (perfume oil) and *oud* (fragrant wood oil), then grab a juice or schwarma at **Ashwaq Cafeteria** (p33) at the corner with Sikkat al Khail St.

❺ Covered Souq

Cut across the intersection and plunge into the tiny alleys of the **Covered Souq** (p40), with shops selling everything from textiles to shisha pipes. It's fun to explore, watch the crowd haggle for deals, and ferret out your own bargain.

❻ Naif Market

Find your way to Al Sabkha Rd and head down 6A St to get to the **Naif Market** (p40), on the site of the historic Naif Souq. Wrap up with a carnivorous feast at **Afghan Khorasan Kabab** (p44), in an adjacent alley next to the Al Ghurair Mosque.

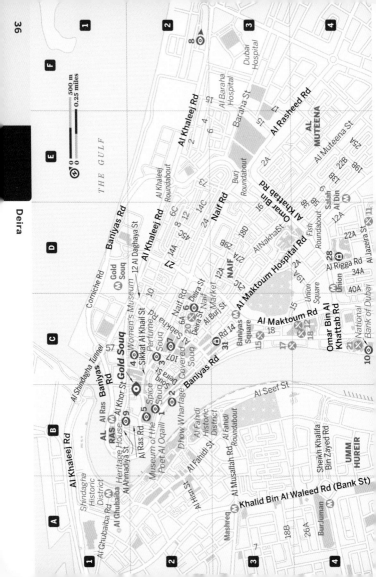

Deira

THE GULF

Al Ghubaiba Rd

Shindagha
Historic
District

Al Khaleej Rd

Al Shindagha Tunnel

**AL
RAS**

Al Ghubaiba Heritage House
Al Ahmadiya St

Corniche Rd

**Baniyas
Rd**

Gold
Souq

Women's Museum

Gold Souq

57

Al Ras

Al Khor St

Al Ras St

Museum of the
Poet Al Oqaili

9

5

1

Spice
Souq

2

Dhow Wharfage

Al Daghaya St

12

Al Khaleej Rd

Al Khaleej
Roundabout

10

Perfume Souq

Sikkat Al Khail St

4

Deira St

Covered
Souq

3

7

107

Baniyas Rd

Naif Rd

Al Sabkha Rd

6A

20

6

Deira St Naif

Al Burj St

Al Market

31

Rd 14

Al Khaleei Rd

2

14A

45C

8

12

14C

6C

Naif Rd

24

Naif Rd

18D

NAIF

12A

27A

29B

2C

Burj
Roundabout

Omar Bin
Al Khattab Rd

Al Nakha St

Fish
Roundabout

Al Maktoum Hospital Rd

2A

19A

15

Union
Square

Banias
Square

15

18

Al Maktoum

17

18

28

Al Rigga Rd

**Omar Bin Al
Khattab Rd**

10

National
Bank of Dubai

Al Jazeira St

11

22A

12A

Salah
Al Din

9

8B

1B

19B

22B

25A

**AL
MUTEENA**

Al Muteena St

Al Rasheed Rd

15

Baraha St

Al Baraha
Hospital

Dubai
Hospital

8

Al Khaleei Rd

Al Barsha Rd

34A

40A

Union

**UMM
HUREIR**

Sheikh Khalifa
Bin Zayed Rd

Al Seef St

Al Fahidi
Historic
District

Al Fahidi
Roundabout

Al Fahidi St

Al Musallah Rd

Al Hisn St

Mashreq

Khalid Bin Al Waleed Rd (Bank St)

7

18B

26A

BurJuman

500 m
0.25 miles

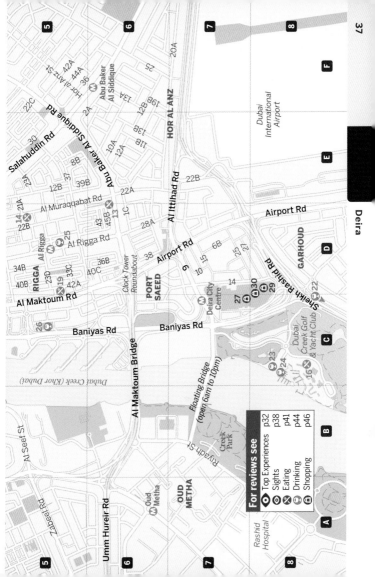

Deira

5
6
7
8

Hor al Anz St
42A
44A
36
**Abu Baker
Al Siddique**
22C
25
20A
13A
19B
12B
2A
HOR AL ANZ
1B
10A
12A

30
Salahuddin Rd
23A
8B
37
39B
12B
Abu Baker Al Siddique Rd
22A
22B

14
21A
22B
Al Muraqqabat Rd
43
45B
13
1C
28A
Al Ittihad Rd

Al Rigga
25
Al Rigga Rd
38
Airport Rd
6
6B
25
27
GARHOUD

*Dubai
International
Airport*

34B
23D
33C
36B
40C
10
15
14
27
30
29

RIGGA
40B
42A
19
**Clock Tower
Roundabout**
**Deira City
Centre**
Sheikh Rashid Rd
22

26
Al Maktoum Rd
**PORT
SAEED**

Baniyas Rd
Baniyas Rd
23
24

*Dubai
Creek Golf
& Yacht Club*

Dubai Creek (Khor Dubai)

Al Maktoum Bridge

**Floating
Bridge**
(open 6am to 10pm)

Al-Seef St
Zabeel Rd

Umm Hureir Rd

Riyadh St

*Creek
Park*

**OUD
METHA**
Oud
Metha

*Rashid
Hospital*

A
B
C
D
E
F

5
6
7
8

For reviews see
● Top Experiences   p32
◉ Sights   p38
✕ Eating   p41
◐ Drinking   p44
▣ Shopping   p46

Travelling Dubai Creek

What the Tiber is to Rome and the Thames is to London, the Creek is to Dubai: a defining stretch of water at the heart of the city. Known as Al Khor in Arabic, the Creek was the base of local fishing and pearling industries in the early 20th century and was dredged in 1961 to allow larger cargo vessels to dock. The first bridge, Al Maktoum, opened two years later.

Four bridges, a tunnel and both Dubai metro lines connect the two banks, but by far the most atmospheric way to get across (especially at or after sunset) is the Dh1 ride aboard a motorised abra. These traditional wooden boats shuttle between the Deira and Bur Dubai souqs in a quick five minutes.

Sights

Spice Souq   MARKET

1 ◉ MAP P36, B2

Steps from the Deira Old Souk abra station, the sound of Arabic chatter bounces around the lanes of this small covered market as vendors work hard to unload cardamom, saffron and other aromatic herbs photogenically stored in burlap sacks alongside nuts, incense burners, henna kits, shishas and dried limes, an essential ingredient in Middle Eastern cuisine.

Away from the tourist-oriented main thoroughfare, the tiny shops also sell groceries, plastics and other household goods to locals and sailors from the dhows (traditional Arabian sailing craft). (btwn Baniyas Rd, Al Ras Rd & Al Abra St; ◷roughly 9am-10pm Sat-Thu, from 4pm Fri; Ⓜ Al Ras)

Dhow Wharfage   HARBOUR

2 ◉ MAP P36, B2

Stroll down the Creek for photogenic close-ups of dozens of brightly coloured dhows docked next to the Deira souqs that load and unload everything from air-conditioners and chewing gum to car tyres. This type of long flat wooden cargo boat has done trade across the Gulf and Indian Ocean for centuries, trading with such countries as Iran, Iraq, India, Somalia and Oman. (along Baniyas Rd; Ⓜ Al Ras)

Perfume Souq   MARKET

3 ◉ MAP P36, C2

Several blocks with a preponderance of perfume shops hardly warrants the title 'souq', yet these stores sell a staggering range of Middle Eastern *attars:* oil-based perfumes that are usually kept in large bulbous bottles and siphoned off into elegant flacons upon purchase. The most precious scents contain *oud,* from a resinous hardwood called agarwood, formed by the southeast Asian aquilaria tree. (Naif Rd & Al Soor St; ⏰10am-1pm & 3-10pm; Ⓜ Gold Souq)

Women's Museum
MUSEUM

4 ◉ MAP P36, C2

Try on a burka (long, enveloping garment), find out about Ousha Bint Khalifa Al Suwaidi (the UAE's most celebrated female poet) and learn about the achievements of local women in the fields of science, trade, education, politics and literature at the region's first museum to train the spotlight on women. The museum is tucked into the warren of lanes north of the Gold Souq and is a bit hard to find. Look for signs in the souq or on Al Khaleej Rd.

(Bait Al Banat; 📞04 234 2342; www.womenmuseumuae.com; Sikka 9 & 28; Dhs20; ⏰10am-7pm Sat-Thu)

Museum of the Poet Al Oqaili
MUSEUM

5 ◉ MAP P36, B2

In 1923 this beautifully restored home tucked into the narrow lanes on the edge of the Spice Souq became the home of Saudi-born Mubarak Bin Al Oqaili (1875–1954), one of the most important classical Arabic poets. A bilingual exhibit charts milestones in his life and work and also displays original manuscripts and personal belongings such as his desk, a gun and a pen. (📞04 515 5000; www.dubaiculture.gov.ae/en; Sikka 21b, Spice Souq; admission free; ⏰8am-2pm Sun-Thu; Ⓜ Al Ras)

Spice Souq

Naif Market MARKET

6 ◉ MAP P36, C2

The historic Naif Souq was burned down in 2008 and replaced by this mall-style version, albeit fronted by arabesque arches. It is especially popular with local women looking for bargain-priced *abayas* (full-length robes) and accessories, such as hair extensions, costume jewellery, *oud* incense and henna products. (btwn Naif South, 9A & Deira Sts; ⊙8.30am-11.30pm; P; MBaniyas Square)

Covered Souq MARKET

7 ◉ MAP P36, C2

Despite the name, this souq is not really covered at all; rather it's an amorphous warren of narrow lanes criss-crossing a few square blocks

roughly bounded by Naif Rd, Al Soor St, 18th St and Al Sabkha Rd. Even if you're not keen on cheap textiles, faux Gucci, *kandouras* (long traditional robes), plastic toys and cheap trainers, you'll likely be entertained by the high-energy street scene. (south of Naif Rd; ⊙9am-10pm; MGold Souq)

Al Mamzar Beach Park BEACH

8 ◉ MAP P36, F2

This lushly landscaped beach park consists of a string of five lovely sandy sweeps and comes with plenty of infrastructure, including a swimming pool, playgrounds, picnic areas with barbecues, water sports and bicycle rentals, snack bars, lawns, Smart Palms for wi-fi access and air-conditioned cabanas (Dhs150 to Dhs200 per day, on

Al Mamzar Beach Park

Getting Off the Main Grid

Easily reached by metro, **Al Muteena St** is one of the most enticing walking streets in town, with wide pavements, palm trees and a park-like strip running along its centre. In the Iraqi restaurants and cafes you'll see *masgouf* – a whole fish sliced in half, seasoned and barbecued over an open flame. The shisha cafes have to be seen to be believed: some feature rock gardens, dangling fronds and artificial lakes. Nearby Al Muraqqabat Rd brims with superb Syrian, Lebanese and Palestinian eateries. A bit south of here, Al Rigga Rd is also packed with promising eateries and also boasts a lively street scene.

Beach 4). (☑04 296 6201; Al Mamzar Creek; per person/car Dhs5/30, pool adult/child Dhs10/5; ⊗8am-10pm Sun-Wed, to 11pm Thu-Sat; Ⓟ)

Heritage House   MUSEUM

 9 ◉ MAP P36, B1

Closed for renovation at the time of writing, this 1890 courtyard house once belonged to Sheikh Ahmed Bin Dalmouk, a wealthy pearl merchant and founder of the adjacent Al Ahmadiya School. Built from coral and gypsum, it wraps around a central courtyard flanked by verandas to keep direct sunlight out, and sports lofty wind towers for cooling the air. (☑04 226 0286; www.dubaiculture.gov.ae/en; Al Ahmadiya St; ⓂAl Ras)

National Bank of Dubai   ARCHITECTURE

10 ◉ MAP P36, C4

In 2007 the National Bank of Dubai merged with Emirates Bank to form Emirates NBD, but its head-quarters remains in this shim-mering landmark overlooking the Creek. Designed by Carlos Ott and completed in 1997, it combines simple shapes to represent a dhow with a billowing sail, while the real-life dhows plying the Creek are reflected in its gold-coated glass facade. Best at sunset. (Emirates NBD; Baniyas Rd; ⓂUnion)

Eating

Aroos Damascus   SYRIAN $

11 ⊗ MAP P36, D4

A Dubai restaurant serving Syrian food to adoring crowds since 1980 must be doing something right. A perfect meal would start with hummus and a *fattoush* salad of toasted bread, tomatoes, onions and mint leaves before moving on to a plate of succulent grilled kebabs. There's a huge outdoor patio. This spot is busy until the wee hours. (☑04 221 9825; cnr Al Muraqqabat Rd & Al Jazeira St;

sandwiches Dhs4-20, mezze Dhs14-35, mains Dhs15-50; ⏱7am-3am; Ⓜ Salah Al Din)

Aseelah

EMIRATI $$

12 🍴 MAP P36, C4

With its mix of traditional and modern Emirati cuisine, this stylish restaurant ticks all the boxes. Many dishes feature a local spice mix called *bezar* (containing cumin, fennel, cinnamon and dried chillies), including the date-stuffed chicken leg and camel stew. To go the whole, well, goat, order *ouzi*, an entire animal filled with legumes and nuts, slow-cooked for 24 hours. Snag a table on the terrace for sublime Creek views. (📞04 205 7033; www.radissonblu.com; Baniyas Rd, 2nd fl, Radisson Blu Hotel, Al Rigga; mains Dhs50-195; ⏱12.30-4pm & 6.30-11.15pm; Ⓟ 🛜; Ⓜ Union, Baniyas Square)

Al Tawasol

YEMENI $

13 🍴 MAP P36, D6

Camp out on the carpet in the main dining room or in a private 'Bedouin-style tent' at this traditional Yemeni eatery. Staff will spread a flimsy plastic sheet to protect the rug from earthy dishes such as turmeric-laced rice topped with curried mutton, oven-roasted chicken *mandi* (rice topped with spicy stew) or an entire sheep if you're really peckish (Dhs800). (📞04 295 9797; Abu Bakar Al Siddique Rd, Al Rigga; mains Dhs25-75; ⏱11am-1am; Ⓜ Al Rigga)

Qwaider Al Nabulsi

MIDDLE EASTERN $

14 🍴 MAP P36, D5

Behind the garish neon facade, this place at first looks like a sweet shop (the *kunafeh,* a vermicelli-like pastry soaked in syrup, is great), but it also has a full menu of Middle Eastern delicacies like scrumptious *musakhan* (chicken pie) and sesame-seed-coated falafel *mahshi* (stuffed with chilli paste). The latter's fluffy filling is coloured green from the addition of parsley and other herbs. (📞04 227 7760; Al Muraqqabat St; snacks Dhs10-17, mains Dhs28-50; ⏱8am-2am; 👫; Ⓜ Al Rigga, Salah Al Din)

Xiao Wei Yang Hotpot

MONGOLIAN $$

15 🍴 MAP P36, C3

Next to Twin Towers, this authentic hotpot restaurant works like this: a tasty bubbling broth inspired by Genghis Khan is placed on a hot plate on your table. Create a dipping sauce from a mix of satay, garlic, coriander, chilli and spices. Choose ingredients (fish balls, tofu, shiitake mushrooms, lotus root, beef slices) to cook in the cauldron. Dip and enjoy!

Note that there is little English spoken, and little atmosphere. No worries, you are here for the food! (Little Lamb Mongolian Hotpot; 📞04 221 5111; www.facebook.com/xiaoweiyangdubai; Baniyas Rd; hotpots Dhs28-32, meats Dhs36-48, combos Dhs98-148; ⏱11am-1am; Ⓜ Baniyas Square)

Thai Kitchen THAI $$

16 🍴 MAP P36, C8

The decor is decidedly un-Thai, with black-lacquer tables, a swooping wave-form ceiling and not a branch of bamboo. Led by respected Thai chef Supattra Boonsrang since 2005, the cooks here know their stuff: dishes are inspired by Bangkok street eats and served in sizes that are perfect for grazing and sharing. The view of the Creek is tops too. (📞04 602 1234; www.dubai.park.hyatt.com; Dubai Creek Club St, Park Hyatt Dubai; small plates Dhs42-70, Sat brunch Dhs255-395; ⏱noon-11.45pm; 🅿🛜🍸; Ⓜ City Centre Deira)

Al Mansour Dhow INTERNATIONAL $$$

17 🍴 MAP P36, C3

Take in the skyline on this moving feast aboard a traditional wooden dhow (cargo boat) decorated with bands of twinkling lights. Soulful Arabic song accompanies the lavish buffet spread that includes Middle Eastern and Western choices (including a live pasta station). There's a full bar and an upper-deck shisha lounge for chilling. Board outside the Radisson Blu Hotel, which operates this dinner cruise. (📞04 205 7033; www.radissonblu.com; Baniyas Rd, Radisson Blu Hotel; 2hr dinner cruise adult/child Dhs185/100; ⏱8pm; 🅿🛜; Ⓜ Union, Baniyas Square)

Falafel on a bed of hummus

Shabestan
IRANIAN $$$

18 MAP P36, C4

This long-standing traditional Persian lair has unpretentious decor and a lovely panorama of glittering lights unfolding over the Creek. Take your sweet time as you tuck into classics such as *fesenjan ba morgh* (chicken in walnut and pomegranate sauce) or *ghormeh sabzi* (lamb stew) and finish up with a scoop of vermicelli ice cream with saffron and rose water. (📞04 222 7171; www.radissonblu.com; Baniyas Rd, Radisson Blu Hotel; mains Dhs105-185; ⏱12.30-3pm & 7-11pm; P 🛜; Ⓜ Union, Baniyas Square)

Sadaf Iranian Sweets
DESSERTS $

19 ✕ MAP P36, D5

Tucked into a small arcade, this little shop brims with spices, nuts, saffron, tea and other goodies from Iran, but insiders flock here for *faloodeh,* a mouth-watering dessert consisting of crunchy vermicelli-sized noodles drenched in a syrup made from rose water, lemon and sugar and served with a scoop of saffron ice cream. (📞04 229 7000; Rigga Al Buteen Plaza, Al Maktoum Rd; sweets Dhs20-30; ⏱8am-midnight; Ⓜ Al Rigga)

Afghan Khorasan Kabab
AFGHANI $

20 ✕ MAP P36, C2

Big hunks of meat – mutton or chicken – charred on foot-long skewers are paired with Afghan *pulao* (rice pilaf), chewy bread and homemade hot sauce. That's it. For added authenticity, eat with your hands and sit upstairs in the carpeted *majlis* (reception room). It's in an alley behind Al Ghurair Mosque. (📞04 338 9838; off Deira St; mains Dhs19-40; ⏱11.30am-1am; Ⓜ Baniyas Square)

Ashiana
INDIAN $$$

21 ✕ MAP P36, C4

This oldie but goodie serves modernised Indian fare in an elegant, dimly lit dining room that radiates the intimacy of an old private villa. The menu spans the arc from richly nuanced curries and succulent kebabs to fluffy biryanis and inspired shareable mains such as *raan lucknowi* (slow-cooked, 48-hour marinated lamb), all beautifully presented. (📞04 207 1733; www.ashianadubai.com; Baniyas Rd, ground fl, Sheraton Dubai Creek Hotel & Towers; mains Dhs58-148; ⏱noon-3pm & 7-11pm; 🛜 🛅; Ⓜ Union)

Drinking

Irish Village
IRISH PUB

22 🕐 MAP P36, C8

This always-buzzing pub, with its Irish-main-street facade (complete with post office) and made with materials imported straight from the Emerald Isle, has been a Dubai institution since 1996. There's Guinness and Kilkenny on tap, lovely gardens around a petite lake, the occasional live band and plenty of pub grub to keep those tummy rumblings at bay. (📞04 282 4750; www.theirishvillage.com; 31A St, Garhoud; ⏰11am-1am Sun-Wed, to 2am Thu-Sat; 📶; MGGICO)

QDs

BAR

23 🚇 MAP P36, C8

Watch the ballet of lighted dhows floating by while sipping cocktails at this always-fun outdoor Creek-side lounge deck where carpets and cushions set an inviting mood. In summer, keep cool in an air-conditioned tent. Great for shisha-holics too. (📞04 295 6000; www.dubaigolf.com; Dubai Creek Club St, Dubai Creek Golf & Yacht Club, Garhoud; shisha Dhs65; ⏰5pm-2am Sun-Wed, to 3am Thu & Sat, 1pm-3am Fri; 📶; MCity Centre Deira)

Cielo
Sky Lounge

BAR

24 🚇 MAP P36, C8

Looking very much like a futuristic James Bond–worthy yacht, Cielo flaunts a sultry, romantic vibe helped by the bobbing yachts below and the cool views of the Dubai skyline across the Creek. One of the chicest spots on this side of town to ring in the night with sundowners and global bar bites. On the downside, the bar staff can be surly. (📞04 416 1800; www.cielodubai.com; Dubai Creek Club St, Dubai Creek Golf & Yacht Club; ⏰4pm-2am Sep-May; 📶; MCity Centre Deira)

QDs

Juice World JUICE BAR

25 🚇 MAP P36, D5

Need some A.S.S., Man Kiwi or Viagra? Then head down to this actually very wholesome Saudi juice bar famous not only for its 200 fantastically creative liquid potions but also for its outrageous fruit sculptures. There's an entire room of them: it must be seen to be believed. The big outdoor terrace offers primo people-watching. (📞04 299 9465; www.juiceworld.ae; Al Rigga St; ⏰10am-3am Sat-Wed, from 2pm Thu & Fri; Ⓜ Al Rigga)

Issimo SPORTS BAR

26 🚇 MAP P36, C5

Illuminated blue flooring, black-leather sofas and sleek chrome finishing lend an edgy look to this sports-and-martini bar. If you're not into sports – or TV – you may find the giant screens a tad distracting, but if you are here to catch a game, it's ace. (📞04 227 1111; www.3hilton.com; Baniyas Rd, Hilton Dubai Creek; ⏰3pm-1am; 📶; Ⓜ Al Rigga, Union)

Shopping

City Centre Deira MALL

27 🔒 MAP P36, C7

Though other malls are bigger and flashier, City Centre Deira remains a stalwart for its logical layout and wide selection of shops, from big-name chains like H&M

and Zara to locally owned stores carrying quality carpets, souvenirs and handicrafts. (📞04 295 1010; www.citycentredeira.com; Baniyas Rd; ⏰10am-10pm Sun-Wed, to midnight Thu-Sat; 📶; Ⓜ City Centre Deira)

Al Ghurair Centre MALL

28 🔒 MAP P36, D4

Dubai's oldest shopping mall opened in 1980 and is a lot less flashy than its newer cousins, despite an expansion that doubled its number of shops to 390. Aside from the expected Western labels, there are speciality stores selling national dress and Middle Eastern fragrances. There's also a food court with 70 outlets and an 18-screen multiplex. (📞800 24227; www.alghuraircentre.com; cnr Al Rigga & Omar Bin Al Khattab Rds; ⏰10am-10pm Sun-Wed, to midnight Thu-Sat; Ⓜ Union, Salah Al Din, Al Rigga)

Mikyajy COSMETICS

29 🔒 MAP P36, D8

You feel like you're walking into a chocolate gift-box at tiny Mikyajy, the region's home-grown makeup brand. Although calibrated to Middle Eastern tastes and complexions, the vivid colours will brighten up any face. (📞04 295 7844; www.mikyajy.com; Baniyas Rd, 2nd fl, City Centre Deira; ⏰10am-10pm Sun-Wed, to midnight Thu-Sat; 📶; Ⓜ City Centre Deira)

A Primer on Bargaining

o Compare prices at a few shops or stalls so you get an idea of what things cost and how much you're willing to pay.

o When you're interested in buying an item, don't show too much enthusiasm or you'll never get the price down.

o Don't pay the first price quoted. This is actually considered arrogant.

o Start below the price you wish to pay so you have room to compromise – but don't quote too low or the vendor may feel insulted. A good rule of thumb is to cut the first suggested price in half and go from there. Expect to finish up with a discount of 20% to 30%.

o If you intend to buy more than one item, use this as a bargaining chip – the more you buy, the better the discount.

o Take your time and stay relaxed. You can come away with an enjoyable experience whether you end up with a bargain or not.

o If negotiations aren't going to plan, simply smile and say goodbye – often the vendor will follow and suggest a compromise price.

Damas Collections JEWELLERY

30 MAP P36, D8

Founded in 1907, Damas may not be the most innovative jeweller in Dubai, but with more than 50 shops, it's essentially omnipresent. Among the diamonds and gold, look for elaborate bridal jewellery as well as classic pieces and big-designer names such as Fabergé and Tiffany. (☏04 295 3848; www.damasjewellery.com; Baniyas Rd, City Centre Deira; ⏰10am-10pm Sun-Wed, to midnight Thu-Sat; 🛜; Ⓜ City Centre Deira)

Gift Village DEPARTMENT STORE

31 🔒 MAP P36, C3

If you've spent all your money on Jimmy Choo shoes and bling at the Gold Souq and need a new in-flight bag, this cut-price place has a great range. It also stocks cosmetics, shoes, clothing, toys, sports goods, jewellery and amiably kitsch souvenirs, all imported from China, Thailand and Turkey. (☏04 294 6858; www.gift-village.com; 14th St, Baniyas Sq; ⏰9am-1am Sun-Thu, 9am-noon & 2pm-2am Fri; Ⓜ Baniyas Square)

ABRA NO.
92

65

Explore ⊛
Bur Dubai

Historic Bur Dubai provides an eye-opening journey back in time, with its most intriguing areas hugging the waterfront. Delve into the city's past in the Al Fahidi and Shindagha historic areas and Dubai Museum, then watch the abras (traditional wooden ferries) depart for quick cross-Creek rides to the Deira souqs. The streets of the surrounding Meena Bazaar district are nirvana for adventurous foodies and also harbour a bustling souq that trades in textiles. For a special treat, book ahead for a meal hosted by the Sheikh Mohammed Centre for Cultural Understanding to meet locals and eat home-cooked Emirati food.

Away from the Creek, Bur Dubai becomes rather nondescript, if not without its highlights. Near upmarket BurJuman mall, densely populated Karama offers great bargain shopping and more bustling eateries serving princely meals at pauper prices. It segues into Zabeel Park, one of the city's largest patches of green and home to the Dubai Frame observation tower. The most eye-catching structures further east are the Egyptian-themed Wafi Mall and the pyramid-shaped Raffles hotel.

Getting There & Around
Dubai Metro's Red and Green Lines intersect at BurJuman, with the latter continuing into historic Bur Dubai before crossing the Creek to Deira. The main stops are Mashreq and Al Ghubaiba. Abras link Bur Dubai to Deira from two stations near the Bur Dubai Souq.

Neighbourhood Map on p56

Abra crossing Dubai Creek BENNYMARTY/GETTY IMAGES ©

Top Experience 📸
Look and Learn at Dubai Museum

This museum is your ticket to learning about Dubai's turbo-evolution from fishing and pearling village to global centre of commerce, finance and tourism. It's housed in the Al Fahidi Fort, built around 1800 and considered the oldest surviving structure in town. A walk-through mock souq, exhibits on Bedouin life, and a room highlighting the importance of the sea illustrate the pre-oil era.

◎ MAP P56, E2

📞 04 353 1862

Al Fahidi St

adult/child Dhs3/1

🕐 8.30am-8.30pm Sat-Thu, from 2.30pm Fri

Ⓜ Mashreq

Al Fahidi Fort

Built from coral and limestone and fortified by three towers, the crenellated citadel (pictured) had not only defensive purposes but also served as the residence of the local rulers until 1896. It was then turned into an arsenal for the fledgling city's artillery and weapons and also went through a stint as a prison. The fort is depicted on the 100-dirham note.

Courtyard

The fort is entered via a sturdy teak door festooned with brass spikes that leads to the central courtyard dotted with bronze cannons, traditional wooden fishing boats and traditional dwellings. Other doors lead to modest displays of instruments and handcrafted weapons.

Souq Dioramas

In the actual museum, you cross the deck of a dhow to enter a mock souq with life-size dioramas depicting shopkeepers and craftspeople at work, enhanced by light and sound effects, historical photos and grainy documentary footage.

Pearl-Diving Exhibit

Learn how pearl divers used only nose clips and leather gloves while descending to extraordinary depths in this fascinating display that incorporates historical footage of divers at work.

Archaeological Finds

The final section showcases finds from ancient settlements at Jumeirah, Al Qusais and other local archaeological sites. Most are believed to have been established here between 2000 and 1000 BCE.

★ **Top Tips**

○ Visit early in the morning or late in the afternoon to avoid tour groups.

○ Check out the courtyard walls, made with traditional coral and gypsum.

○ Don't bother with a tour guide: exhibits are sufficiently well explained in English.

○ Take the kids! They'll love the sound effects, films and detailed dioramas.

○ Skip the gift shop and head for the nearby souq instead.

✗ **Take a Break**

For a healthy breakfast or light meal, head to the courtyard of the atmospheric **XVA Café** (📞04 353 5383; www.xvahotel.com/cafe; Al Fahidi Historic District, off Al Fahidi St; dishes Dhs25-55; 🕐7am-10pm; 📶🌿; Ⓜ️Mashreq).

The best butter chicken is served at Sind Punjab (p62), the oldest family eatery in the nearby Indian-dominated Meena Bazaar quarter.

Top Experience 📷
Wander Through Al Fahidi Historic District

Traffic fades to a quiet hum in the labyrinthine lanes of this restored heritage area, formerly known as the Bastakia Quarter. Today, there are about 50 buildings containing crafts shops, cultural exhibits, courtyard cafes, art galleries and two boutique hotels. Above it all rises the distinctive ornate flat dome and slender minaret of the alabaster-white Diwan Mosque.

◉ MAP P56, F2

Al Fahidi St

Ⓜ Mashreq

Alserkal Cultural Foundation

At this dynamic **cultural space** (📞04 353 5922; www.alserkalculturalfoundation.com; Heritage House No 13, off Al Fahidi St; admission free; ⏰9am-7pm; Ⓜ️Mashreq) galleries showcase traditional and cutting-edge works by local and international artists in rooms orbiting a central courtyard with an arty cafe. Most of the art is for sale and there's also a small shop stocking gifts.

Coffee Museum

This cute private **museum** (📞04 353 8777; www.coffeemuseum.ae; Al Fahidi Historical District, off Al Fahidi St; admission free; ⏰9am-5pm Sat-Thu; Ⓜ️Mashreq) in a historic Emirati home offers an aromatic bean-based journey around the world and back in time. You can even sample freshly brewed Ethiopian coffee prepared by staff in traditional garb (Dhs10).

Majlis Gallery

Dubai's oldest **fine art gallery** (📞04 353 6233; www.themajlisgallery.com; Al Fahidi St; admission free; ⏰10am-6pm Sat-Thu; Ⓜ️Mashreq) presents mainly paintings and sculpture by international artists inspired by the region, as well as high-quality pottery, glass and other crafts. It was founded in 1989 by British expat Allison Collins who first came to Dubai in 1976. Renowned Emirati artist Abdul Qader Al Rais had one of his first exhibits here.

Coin Museum

This petite **museum** (📞04 392 0093; www.dubaiculture.gov.ae/en; Al Fahidi Historical District; admission free; ⏰8am-2pm Sun-Thu; Ⓜ️Mashreq) presents nearly 500 rare coins from throughout the Middle East, including Egypt, Turkey and Morocco. The oldest were minted during the Arab-Sasanian era in the 7th century.

★ Top Tips

○ Don't be shy about pushing open some of those heavy doors and finding out what's behind them.

○ Shutterbugs should visit early in the morning or late in the afternoon for the best light conditions.

○ Look for a short section of the old city wall from 1800, which looks a bit like a dinosaur tail.

○ Admission to all museums and exhibits is free.

✕ Take a Break

Have a mint lemonade or snack at the charming courtyard cafe of the Alserkal Cultural Foundation.

Relax in the sun-dappled garden of the Arabian Tea House (p62).

Walking Tour 🥾

Bur Dubai Waterside Walk

This heritage walk of Dubai's oldest area kicks off in the Al Fahidi Historic District, where you can wander around the atmospheric narrow lanes and peek into the renovated wind-tower houses. From here the route ticks off several of Dubai's most interesting traditional sights along the Creek and provides a glimpse into the pre-oil era with nary a shopping mall, skyscraper or ski slope in sight.

Walk Facts

Start Al Fahidi Historic District

End Saruq Al Hadid Archaeology Museum

Length 3km; two to three hours

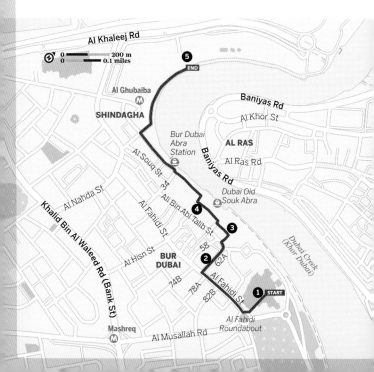

❶ Al Fahidi Historic District

Kick off your tour with a leisurely wander along the narrow lanes of one of Dubai's oldest **neighbourhoods** (p52) and check out the traditional wind-tower architecture. Pop into small museums like the **Coffee Museum** (p53) or galleries like **XVA Gallery** (p60) and the **Alserkal Cultural Foundation** (p53) before stopping for refreshments in the enchanting walled garden of the **Arabian Tea House** (p62).

❷ Dubai Museum

Wrap up the historic district by checking out the **Majlis Gallery** (p53), the oldest art space in Dubai, before continuing west along Al Fahidi St to the **Dubai Museum** (p50), which introduces the history, heritage and development of this burgeoning city. Turn left as you exit the museum and peer towards Dubai's tallest minaret, atop the **Grand Mosque**.

❸ Hindi Lane

Follow the lane to the mosque's right-hand side before ducking into teensy **Hindi Lane** (p61), a vibrant and colourful alley lined with pint-sized shops selling religious paraphernalia. This alley is home to Dubai's only Hindu temple.

❹ Bur Dubai Souq

Exiting Hindi Lane takes you to the wooden arcades of the **Bur Dubai Souq** (p60) and its colourful textile and trinket shops. Lug your loot to the waterfront and snap pictures of the abras at the Dubai Old Souk abra station before following the Creek north to the Shindagha Historic District.

❺ Shindagha Historic District

Lined with the historic former residences of Dubai's ruling family, this waterfront area is undergoing extensive redevelopment. Ignore the dust and make your way to the splendid **Sheikh Saeed Al Maktoum House** (p58) to marvel at the amazing photo collection of old Dubai, then check out the beautifully displayed finds from Dubai's latest desert dig at the **Saruq Al Hadid Archaeology Museum** (p58).

Bur Dubai

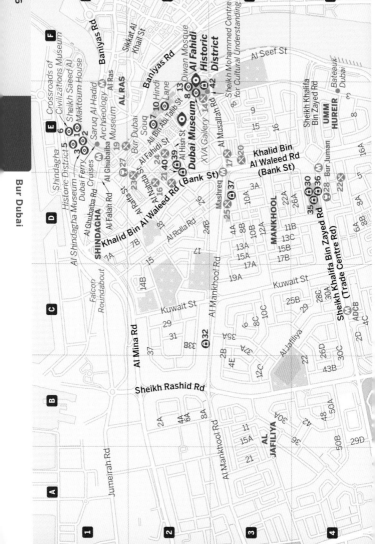

Banyas Rd

Sikkat Al
Khail St

Al Seef St

Baniyas Rd

Diwan Mosque

**Al Fahidi
Historic
District**

Sheikh Mohammed Centre
for Cultural Understanding

**Crossroads of
Civilizations Museum**

Sheikh Saeed Al
Maktoum House

13

AL RAS

Saruq Al Hadid
Archaeology

Al Ghubaiba Museum

Bur Dubai
Souq

7 10 Al
Hindi
Lane

8 Al Fahidi

14 XVA Gallery

Sheikh Khalifa
Bin Zayed Rd

Bateaux
Dubai

42

**UMM
HUREIR**

16

15

9

Al Bin Abu Talib St

Dubai Museum

Al Musallah Rd

16A

Shindagha

Historic District

Al Shindagha Museum

Dubai Ferry
Cruises

Al Ras St

19

27

Al Falah Rd

Al Nahda St

21 40

39

16

23

Al Hisn St

17

20

**Khalid Bin
Al Waleed Rd
(Bank St)**

3A

5

Bur Juman

22

28

SHINDAGHA

Al Ghubaiba Museum

Khalid Bin Al Waleed Rd (Bank St)

7B

Al Rolla Rd

24B

Mashreq

25 37

10A

8B

4A

MANKHOOL

22A

26A

11B

13C

15B

17B

35 30

36

**Sheikh Khalifa Bin Zayed Rd
(Trade Centre Rd)**

6A

6B

8A

**Falcon
Roundabout**

14B

15

7A

Al Mankhool Rd

13A

15A

17A

19A

8B

8C

Kuwait St

25B

29

28C

30A

9

2D

Al Jafiliya

Al Mina Rd

Kuwait St

29

31

37

33B

32

35A

2B

4E

12C

10C

26D

22

30C

43B

ADCB

Sheikh Rashid Rd

Al Mankhool Rd

2A

4A

6A

8A

11

15A

21

**AL
JAFILIYA**

42

50A

36

50B

29D

30A

48

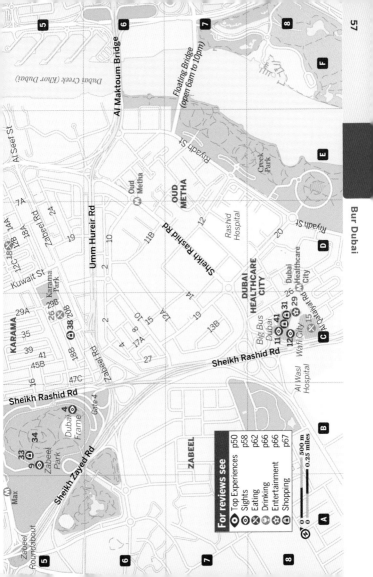

Bur Dubai

Dubai Creek (Khor Dubai)

Al Maktoum Bridge

Floating Bridge
(open 6am to 10pm)

Al Seef St

7A

12C 18B 14A
12B
18A
24
Zabeel Rd
19

Umm Hureir Rd

Kuwait St

Riyadh St

Creek
Park

Oud
Metha

OUD
METHA

11B

12
2
10

Sheikh Rashid Rd

Karama
Park

29A
26
29B
20B

KARAMA

35
38
18B 18B
Zabeel Rd

39
41
45B

16
47C

Rashid
Hospital

20

Riyadh St

14

DUBAI
HEALTHCARE
CITY

15
2
10
12A
19

13B

Big Bus
Dubai
11
41
120
12
31
29
26

Dubai
Healthcare
City

Al Wasi Rd
Wafi City

Sheikh Rashid Rd

27

4
17A
8

Sheikh Rashid Rd

Al Wasi
Hospital

Sheikh Rashid Rd

Zabeel
Roundabout

Max

33
9

34

Zabeel
Park

Dubai
Frame

Gate 4

Sheikh Zayed Rd

ZABEEL

For reviews see

◉	Top Experiences	p50
⊙	Sights	p58
✕	Eating	p62
⊗	Drinking	p66
⊗	Entertainment	p66
⊗	Shopping	p67

500 m
0.25 miles

Sights

Sheikh Saeed Al Maktoum House

MUSEUM

1 MAP P56, E1

Restored as part of the Shindagha Historic District development, this grand courtyard house served as the residence of Sheikh Saeed, the grandfather of current Dubai ruler Sheikh Mohammed Bin Rashid, from 1912 until his death in 1958. Today, the architectural marvel houses an excellent collection of pre–oil boom photographs of Dubai taken in the souqs, on the Creek and at traditional celebrations. There are also some insightful private images of the ruling Al Maktoum clan. (☑04 393 7139; Shindagha Waterfront, Shindagha Historic District; adult/child Dhs3/1; ⏰8am-8.30pm Sat-Thu, 3-9.30pm Fri; Ⓜ Al Ghubaiba)

Saruq Al Hadid Archaeology Museum

MUSEUM

2 MAP P56, E1

Only discovered in 2002, Saruq Al Hadid sits deep in the desert sands of the southern reaches of the Dubai emirate and is believed to have been an iron-age metal 'factory' in operation between 1300 and 800 BCE. Excavations have thus far yielded mostly swords, axe heads, daggers and other weapons, some of which are on display in this modern museum. Videos documenting the site's discovery and featuring interviews with archaeologists about their latest findings and theories provide further insight. (☑ext 203 04 359 5612; www.saruq alhadid.ae; Shindagha Waterfront; adult/child Dhs20/10; ⏰8am-8pm Sun-Wed, to 2pm Thu & Sat; Ⓜ Al Ghubaiba)

Explore Emirati Culture

Open doors, open minds: such is the motto of the **Sheikh Mohammed Centre for Cultural Understanding** (☑04 353 6666; www.cultures.ae; House 26, Al Musallah Rd; heritage/Creekside tours Dhs80/275, meals Dhs90-120; ⏰9am-5pm Sun-Thu, to 1pm Sat; Ⓟ; Ⓜ Mashreq), an institution founded by Dubai's ruler Sheikh Mohammed bin Rashid in 1998 to help visitors understand the traditions and customs of the United Arab Emirates. It conducts guided tours of the Al Fahidi Historic District and Jumeirah Mosque and also hosts hugely popular cultural breakfasts and lunches where you also get a chance to meet, ask questions of, and exchange ideas with Emiratis. Reservations essential.

KATIEKK/SHUTTERSTOCK ©

Dubai Frame

Al Shindagha Museum

MUSEUM

3  MAP P56, E1

A focal point of the upgraded historic Shindagha waterfront, this museum peels back the layers of Dubai's history and heritage through artefacts, art, photographs, video and events. (☏800 33222; https://alshindagha.dubai culture.gov.ae; Shindagha Waterfront; adult/student Dhs15/5; ⊙10am-5pm Wed-Mon, last entry 4pm; Ⓜ Al Ghubaiba)

Dubai Frame

VIEWPOINT

4  MAP P56, B5

This 150m rectangular 'picture frame' sits in Zabeel Park (p60), right between historic and modern Dubai, and provides grand views of both parts of the city. Galleries on the ground floor tell the story of Dubai (the past) before visitors are whisked up to a viewing platform at roof level (the present). The final stop is another gallery depicting a vision of Dubai 50 years from now (the future). (www.thedubaiframe. com; Gate 3, Zabeel Park; adult/child Dhs50/20; ⊙9am-9pm; Ⓜ Max)

Shindagha Historic District

AREA

5  MAP P56, E1

Strategically located at the mouth of Dubai Creek, Shindagha was where the ruling sheikhs and the city elite lived until the 1950s. A few of the homes have been reconstructed and recast as museums including Sheikh Saeed Al

Maktoum House (p58) and Saruq
Al Hadid Archaeology Museum
(p58). The area now also hosts
the impressive Al Shindagha Museum (p59) as well as additional
exhibits, heritage hotels, cafes
and restaurants. It enjoys a lovely
position on the Creek and remains
very quiet. (Shindagha Waterfront;
Ⓜ Al Ghubaiba)

Crossroads of Civilizations Museum
MUSEUM

6 ◉ MAP P56, E1

This private museum in the
Shindagha Historic District (p59)
provides a fascinating glimpse of
Dubai's historic role as a trading
link between East and West. On
display are hundreds of artefacts
from the Ubaids, Greeks, Romans,
Babylonians and other civilisations
that passed through the region.
(☎ 04 393 4440; www.themuseum.
ae; Al Khaleej Rd; Dhs30; ⏱ 9am-5pm
Sat-Thu; Ⓜ Al Ghubaiba)

Bur Dubai Souq
MARKET

7 ◉ MAP P56, E2

Dubai's oldest souq (market)
flanks a central arcade canopied
by an ornately carved wooden
roof. Friday evenings here are
especially lively, as it turns into
a virtual crawling carnival with
expat workers loading up on socks,
pashminas, T-shirts and knock-
off Calvins. In a section known as
the **Textile Souq** you can stock
up on fabrics – silk, cotton, satin
and velvet – at very reasonable

prices. On the downside, although
good humoured, the vendors
here can be very pushy. (btwn Bur
Dubai waterfront & Ali Bin Abi Talib St;
⏱ 8am-1pm & 4-10pm Sat-Thu, 4-10pm
Fri; Ⓜ Al Ghubaiba)

XVA Gallery
GALLERY

8 ◉ MAP P56, E2

Tucked into the Al Fahidi Historic
District (p52) since 2003, XVA
has a knack for ferreting out
top-notch up-and-comers from
around the Middle East and India.
Works often express the artists'
cultural identities and challenge
viewers' preconceptions. It also
participates in prestigious art fairs
such as Art Basel and Art London
and holds regular art courses.
(☎ 04 353 5383; www.xvagallery.com;
XVA Guesthouse, Al Fahidi Historic
District, off Al Fahidi St; ⏱ 10am-6pm;
Ⓜ Mashreq)

Zabeel Park
PARK

9 ◉ MAP P56, B5

This sprawling park, where lots of
palms and other greenery provide
plenty of shade, is a weekend family favourite. It brims with activity
zones, including a pretty lake with
boat rides, an adventure playground, covered barbecue areas, a
jogging track and a miniature train.
It is also home to the Dubai Frame
(p59). (☎ 04 398 6888; Gate 1, off
Sheikh Khalifa Bin Zayed Rd; Dhs5;
⏱ 8am-10pm Sun-Wed, to 11pm Thu-
Sat; 🚻; Ⓜ Max)

The History of Al Fahidi

Previously known as Bastakia Quarter, the Al Fahidi Historic District was built in the early 1900s by merchants from the Persian town of Bastak, who settled in Dubai to take advantage of tax breaks granted by the sheikh. By the 1970s, though, the buildings had fallen into disrepair and residents began moving on to newer, more comfortable neighbourhoods. Dedicated locals, expats and even Prince Charles prevented the area's demolition in the 1980s. To learn more, sign up for a guided tour with the Sheikh Mohammed Centre for Cultural Understanding (p58).

Hindi Lane   STREET

10 ◉ MAP P56, E2

This narrow and colourful alleyway colloquially known as Hindi Lane is lined with vendors selling religious paraphernalia and offerings, including baskets of fruit, flower garlands and sacred ash and sandalwood paste. Via this alleyway, you reach a tiny and ageing double-shrine, dedicated to Shiva and Krishna, that has been tucked behind the Grand Mosque since 1958 and serves the UAE's nearly three million Hindus. (off Ali Bin Abi Talib St; Ⓜ Mashreq, Al Ghubaiba)

Big Bus Dubai   BUS

11 ◉ MAP P56, C8

These hop-on, hop-off city tours aboard open-topped double-decker buses are a good way for Dubai first-timers to get their bearings. Buses with recorded commentary in several languages run on three interlinking routes, making 35 stops at major malls, beaches and landmarks. Passes also include extras such as a dhow cruise, a night bus tour and museum admissions. Tickets are sold online (10% discount), on the bus or at hotels. (☏ 04 340 7709; www.bigbustours.com; day pass adult/child Dhs273/174)

Wafi City   AREA

12 ◉ MAP P56, C8

Ancient Egypt gets a Dubai-style makeover at this lavishly designed hotel, residential, restaurant and shopping complex, complete with pyramids, hieroglyphs and statues of Ramses and Anubis. The best time to visit is during the sound-and-light-show that kicks off nightly at 9.30pm (September to May). In the cooler months, free outdoor movie screenings take over the Rooftop Gardens on Sunday nights at 8.30pm.

Wafi City was created in the 1990s and was one of the emirate's first new modern districts that combined entertainment, leisure, shopping and living. (☏ 04 324 4555; www.wafi.com; Oud Metha

& Sheikh Rashid Rds; **P**; **M** Dubai Healthcare City)

Diwan Mosque   MOSQUE

13 ◎ MAP P56, E2

The distinctive ornate flat dome and slender minaret of this snowy white mosque watch over the Al Fahidi Historic District (p52). Non-Muslims may only visit the interior on guided tours offered by the Sheikh Mohammed Centre for Cultural Understanding (p58). (Al Mussalah St; **M** Mashreq)

Eating

Arabian Tea House   CAFE $$

14 ✖ MAP P56, E2

A grand old tree, white wicker chairs, turquoise benches and crimson bougainvillea create a sun-dappled refuge in the court-yard of an old pearl merchant's house. The menu includes Emirati specialities, including *raqaq* (tra-ditional bread), chicken *machboos* (spicy casserole with rice) and *sa-loona* chicken (in a tomato-based stew). Its traditional breakfast also comes highly recommended, but only if you are truly hungry. (☑04 353 5071; www.arabianteahouse. co; Al Fahidi St; breakfast Dhs30-65, mains Dhs48-65; ⏰7.30am-10pm; 🛜; **M** Mashreq)

Tomo   JAPANESE $$$

15 ✖ MAP P56, C8

The name of this gorgeously for-mal restaurant translates as 'long-

time friend', which is quite apropos given its league of loyal followers. No gimmicky fusion here, just Japanese cuisine at its best: super-fresh sushi and sashimi, delectable Wagyu beef, feathery tempura and other treasured morsels. Plus dazzling views from the 360-degree terrace on the 17th floor of the Raffles hotel. (☑04 357 7888; www.tomo.ae; 13th St, 17th fl, Raffles Dubai, Wafi City; mains Dhs70-550; ⏰12.30-3.30pm & 6.30pm-1am; **P** 🛜; **M** Dubai Healthcare City)

Sind Punjab   INDIAN $

16 ✖ MAP P56, D2

Like a fine wine, some restaurants only get better over time and such is the case with Sind Punjab, the first family eatery to open in Meena Bazaar in 1977. It still has a feverish local following for its finger-lickin' northern Indian specialities like butter chicken and *dal makhani* (a rich black-lentil and kidney-bean stew). (☑04 352 5058; cnr Al Esbij & 29A Sts; mains Dhs15-38; ⏰8.30am-2am; 🖋; **M** Mashreq, Al Ghubaiba)

Al Ustad
Special Kabab   IRANIAN $

17 ✖ MAP P56, E3

Sheikhs to shoe shiners clutter this funky, been-here-forever (since 1978, to be precise) kebab joint formerly known as Special Ostadi. Amid walls plastered with photographs of cheerful guests, a fleet of swift and quirky servers brings heaped plates of rice and yoghurt-marinated chicken into a dining room humming with chatter and laughter. (📞04 397 1933; Al Musallah Rd; mains Dhs25-42; 🕐noon-4pm & 6.30pm-1am Sat-Thu, 6.30pm-1am Fri; Ⓜ Mashreq)

Eric's

INDIAN $

18 🍽 MAP P56, D5

Prints by Goan cartoonist Mario Miranda decorate the simple, buzzing dining room of this purveyor of magically spiced dishes from the tropical Indian state of Goa. The menu has few false notes, but popular items include the chicken 'lollipops' (drumsticks), the Bombay duck (actually a fish!) and the chicken *xacuti*, a mouth-watering curry with poppy seeds. (📞04 396 5080; 10B St, Sheikh Hamdan Colony, Karama; mains

Dhs20-40; 🕐11.30am-3.30pm & 6.30pm-midnight; 🥢; Ⓜ BurJuman, ADCB)

Saravana Bhavan

INDIAN $

19 🍽 MAP P56, E1

Head a block back from the Bur Dubai Abra Station to find this superb no-frills place, one of the best South Indian vegetarian restaurants in town and one of a chain that extends to New York's Lexington Ave. The vast menu includes wonderfully buttery *palak paneer*, creamy rogan josh, fragrant biryanis and other staples. (📞04 353 9988; www.saravanabhavan.com; Khalifa Bin Saeed Bldg, 3A St; mains Dhs15-17; 🕐7am-11pm Sat-Wed, to 11.30pm Thu & Fri; 🥢; Ⓜ Al Ghubaiba)

Bur Dubai Eating

Arabian Tea House

FRANK FELL MEDIA/SHUTTERSTOCK ©

Hitting Old Dubai's Food Trail

For a mouthwatering immersion in Dubai's multiethnic food and culture, book a small-group walking tour with Arva Ahmad of **Frying Pan Adventures** (www.fryingpanadventures.com; tours Dhs350-395). Enjoy five or six exotic nibbles from India, Lebanon or Nepal as either Arva or her sister Farida takes you through the bewildering tangle of Bur Dubai's or Deira's lanes while also feeding you titbits about the food, the restaurants and local life. Check the website for the schedule and to book a tour.

Antique Bazaar   INDIAN $$

20 🍴 MAP P56, E3

Resembling an exotic Mogul palace, Antique Bazaar's decor is sumptuously ornate with carved-wood seats, ivory-inset tables and richly patterned fabrics. Thumbs up to the *machli mirch ka salan* (fish with coconut, tamarind and curry leaves) and the *murgh kaali mirch korma* (chicken curry with spices and cashew nuts). At dinnertime, a music and dance show competes with the food for your attention. (📞04 397 7444; www.antiquebazaar-dubai.com; 132 Khalid Bin Al Waleed Rd, Four Points by Sheraton Bur Dubai, Mankhool; mains Dhs46-130; 🕐12.30pm-3pm & 7.30pm-midnight; P 🛜; Ⓜ Mashreq)

Kabul Darbar   AFGHANI $

21 🍴 MAP P56, D2

Follow Afghan tradition: find a spot on the carpet, order lots of food and eat with your hands. All dishes are served with a soup, bread and salad, making for a filling and tasty meal. There are tables, chairs and cutlery available if you prefer. (📞04 325 0900; Khalid Bin Al Waleed Rd; mains Dhs20-40; 🕐noon-midnight Sat-Thu, 1pm-midnight Fri; Ⓜ Mashreq)

Govinda's   VEGETARIAN $

22 🍴 MAP P56, D4

Jains run this super-friendly, super-healthy, vegetarian Indian restaurant serving 'body-harmonising' sattvic food that uses only fresh, seasonal and organic produce and shuns oil, onion and garlic. Dishes to try include the velvety *paneer makhanwala* (Indian cheese in creamy tomato gravy) and the rich *dal makhani* with lentils and kidney beans. (📞04 396 0088; www.mygovindas.com; 4A St, Karama; mains Dhs30-42; 🕐noon-3.30pm & 7pm-midnight; 🍴; Ⓜ BurJuman)

Nepaliko Sagarmatha   NEPALI $

23 🍴 MAP P56, D2

At this small and basic joint, Nepali expats soothe their homesickness with platters of tasty *momos* (dumplings), including a version filled with 'buff' (buffalo), as well as steaming bowls of *thukpa* (noodle soup). It's a bit set back from the street overlooking a car park. (04 352 2124; Al Fahidi & 11th St; mains Dhs10-25; noon-midnight; Al Ghubaiba)

Vaibhav   INDIAN $

25 MAP P56, E2

This all-veg street-food haven does a roaring trade in *dosas* (savoury wraps), stuffed *parathas* (pan-fried flatbread) and other southern Indian soul food, all prepared in a Bollywood-worthy spectacle. Try it with a cup of spiced masala chai (tea). Busiest at night. It hides out in a nondescript lane off Al Fahidi St opposite the Elegant Corner nuts shop. It's behind the National Bank of Dubai. (04 353 8130; www.vaibhav.ae; Al Fahidi St; snacks Dhs2-20; 7.30am-11pm; ; Al Gubaibha)

Lebanese Village Restaurant   LEBANESE $

25 MAP P56, D3

Look beyond the sun-bleached photos of dishes: the menu may have few surprises but does staples like grills, hummus and *tabbouleh* (salad of tomatoes, parsley, onions and bulgur) dependably well. The best seats are under a shady umbrella on the pavement terrace (more appealing than the bright diner-style interior). Also handy for a takeaway if you're staying in a nearby hotel apartment. It's just to the north of the Mashreq metro. (04 352 2522; Al Mankhool Rd; mains Dhs25-70; noon-2am; Mashreq)

Karachi Darbar   PAKISTANI $

26 MAP P56, C5

A favourite pit stop of expats and Karama Market shoppers with an eye for a biryani bargain, this local chain puts tummies into a state of

Bacchanalian Boating

A memorable way to experience the magic of 'Old Dubai' is during a dinner cruise along the Creek. Gently cruise past historic waterfront houses, sparkling high-rises, jutting wind towers and dhows bound for India or Iran. Dining rooms are air-conditioned and alcohol is served. **Bateaux Dubai** (Map p56, E4; 04 336 6768; www. bateauxdubai.com; 3 St, Al Seef, Dubai Creek; per person 2½hr dinner cruise with/without alcohol Dhs520/415, children Dhs190; 8.30-11pm; ; BurJuman) is a classy choice, especially if food is as important to you as ambience. Indulge in a four-course à la carte feast aboard this stylish contemporary boat with panoramic windows, linen-draped tables and live music.

contentment with a huge menu of Pakistani, Indian and Chinese dishes. Reliable picks include shrimp masala, mutton *kadai* (one pot mutton dish) and butter chicken. It's near Lulu Supermarket. (📞04 334 7272; www.karachidarbar group.com; 33B St, Karama Market; mains Dhs10-30; ⏱6am-2pm Sun-Thu, to 9pm Fri & Sat; Ⓜ ADCB)

Drinking

George & Dragon PUB

27 📍 MAP P56, E1

This quintessential British pub comes with the requisite dartboard, pool table, cheap beer and several sports' screens. Ladies night is Tuesday, cocktail night is Friday and the most popular pub grub? Chicken tikka masala, of course! Located in the Ambassador, Dubai's oldest hotel (since 1971), it's fun, full of character(s) and an amiable place to wind down with a pint. (📞04 393 9444; www. astamb.com; Al Falah Rd, ground fl,

Ambassador Hotel, Meena Bazaar; ⏱noon-3am; Ⓜ Al Ghubaiba)

Rock Bottom Café BAR

28 📍 MAP P56, D4

This been-here-forever Western expat fave has a '70s-era American roadhouse feel, with a cover band blaring out Top 40 hits and a DJ filling in the breaks with gusto. By day, it's a regular cafe serving international soul food, but with a mob of friends and a bottle of tequila gone, it's the quintessential ending to a rollickin' night on the town. (📞04 396 3888; Sheikh Khalifa Bin Zayed Rd, ground fl, Regent Palace Hotel, Karama; ⏱noon-3am; Ⓜ BurJuman)

Entertainment

Movies Under the Stars OUTDOOR CINEMA

29 ⭐ MAP P56, C8

Every Sunday night during the cooler months, clued-in cinephiles invade the rooftop of the Pyramids

---

Enjoying a Mini-cruise

The **Dubai Ferry** (Map p56, E1; 📞800 9090; www.rta.ae; Shindagha Waterfront; adult/child Dhs50/25; ⏱10am-6pm) provides a fun way for visitors to see the city from the water. Boats depart three times daily (11am, 1pm and 6.30pm) for the 90-minute trip from the Al Ghubaiba ferry station to the Dubai Marina station (and vice-versa). The route passes by such landmarks as Port Rashid, the Burj Al Arab and Madinat Jumeirah. Other options from either station include an afternoon-tea trip at 3pm and a sunset cruise at 5pm. The fare for any of these trips is Dhs50 (children Dhs25).

Building, next to the Wafi Mall, to drop into a giant beanbag and enjoy a free classic flick. A great deal for film buffs.

Food and nonalcoholic drinks are available. (☏ 04 324 4100; www. pyramidsrestaurantsatwafi.com; Pyramids Rooftop Gardens, Wafi City; admission free; ☉ 8.30pm Sun Feb–Apr; ☂ ♿; Ⓜ Dubai Healthcare City)

Shopping

BurJuman   SHOPPING CENTRE

30 🔒 MAP P56, D4

Rather than rest on its laurels, Dubai's oldest high-end mall (open since 1992) just keeps reinventing itself. A remodel added some 200 shops (including luxury brands like Dior and Versace), a vast Carrefour supermarket and a 14-screen multiplex cinema. The upstairs food court, Pavilion Gardens, is an attractively designed, fountain-anchored space lidded by a soaring glass ceiling. (☏ 04 352 0222; www.burjuman.com; Sheikh Khalifa Bin Zayed Rd; ☉ 10am-10pm Sun-Thu, to 11pm Fri & Sat; ☂; Ⓜ BurJuman)

Wafi Mall   MALL

31 🔒 MAP P56, C8

At the heart of Egyptian-style Wafi City (p61) district, one of Dubai's most architecturally striking malls is built around three stained-glass pyramids and guarded by two giant statues of Ramses II. Stock up on gifts from around the Arab world in the basement's **Souq**

Khan Murjan, which was modelled after the namesake Baghdad bazaar. (☏ 04 324 4555; www.wafi.com; Oud Metha Rd; ☉ 10am-10pm Sun-Thu, to midnight Fri & Sat; ☂; Ⓜ Dubai Healthcare City)

Fabindia   FASHION & ACCESSORIES

32 🔒 MAP P56, C2

In business since 1950, Fabindia is one of India's biggest retail chains and mostly sells products hand-made by more than 50,000 Indian villagers using traditional skills and techniques. There's a huge selection of fashion, furnishings and handicrafts, including colourful *kurtis* (tunics), elegant shawls, patterned silk cushions and organic teas and chutneys. (☏ 04 398 9633; www.fabindia.com; Nashwan Bldg, Al Mankhool Rd; ☉ 10am-10pm Sat-Thu, from 2pm Fri; Ⓜ ADCB)

Dubai Flea Market   MARKET

33 🔒 MAP P56, B5

Trade malls for stalls and look for bargains amid the piles of preloved stuff that's spilled out of local closets at Dubai's cherished flea markets, which take place every weekend in a different spot around town, including at this great location inside the vast Zabeel Park. Check the website for upcoming markets. (☏ 055 886 8939; www. dubai-fleamarket.com; Gates 1 & 2, Zabeel Park; Dhs5; ☉ 8am-3pm every 1st Sat Oct-May; Ⓜ Max)

Ripe Market   MARKET

34 🔒 MAP P56

This market features not only fruit
and veg from local growers but
also local honey, nuts, spices and
eggs, plus arts and crafts, food stations and locally roasted gourmet
coffee – pretty much all you need
for a picnic under the palms. (📞04
315 7000; www.ripeme.com/the-ripe-
markets; Dubai Police Academy Park,
Umm Suqeim 3; 🕙9am-7pm Fri & Sat
late Oct-Mar; 🛜; Ⓜ Max)

Bateel   FOOD

35 🔒 MAP P56, D4

Old-style traditional Arab hospital-
ity meant dates and camel milk.
Now Emiratis offer their guests Bateel's scrumptious date chocolates
and truffles, made using European

Attar (perfume) for sale

ANDRZEJ KUBIK/SHUTTERSTOCK ©

chocolate-making techniques.
Staff are happy to give you a
sample before you buy. Most other
Dubai malls have their own Bateel
branches; check the website for
details. (📞04 355 2853; www.bateel.
com; Sheikh Khalifa Bin Zayed Rd, 1st fl,
BurJuman; 🕙10am-10pm Sun-Thu, to
11pm Fri & Sat; 🛜; Ⓜ BurJuman)

Ajmal   PERFUME

36 🔒 MAP P56, D4

The place for traditional Middle
Eastern *attars* (perfumes), Ajmal
custom blends its earthy scents
and pours them into fancy gold
or jewel-encrusted bottles. These
aren't frilly French colognes –
they're woody and pungent perfumes. Ask for the signature scent
'Ajmal', based on white musk and
jasmine. (📞04 351 5505; www.
ajmalperfume.com; Sheikh Khalifa
Bin Zayed Rd, BurJuman; 🕙10am-
10pm Sun-Thu, to 11pm Fri & Sat;
Ⓜ BurJuman)

Computer Plaza   ELECTRONICS

37 🔒 MAP P56, D3

Really handy if you have a sudden
hardware/software demand or di-
lemma, this jam-packed computer
and electronics mall has more
than 80 outlets selling every kind
of computer hardware and acces-
sory, including printers and scan-
ners, plus software, mobile phones
and cameras. On the ground floor,
a sandwich place and an ice-cream
counter keep tummy rumblings
in check. (📞055 335 5533, 600
560 609; www.computerplaza-me.

com; Al Mankhool Rd, Al Ain Center;
🕑10am-10pm Sat-Thu, from 2pm Fri;
Ⓜ Mashreq)

Karama Market MARKET

38 🅐 MAP P56, C5

Despite its visually unappeal-
ing concrete exterior, Karama's
bustling backstreet shopping area
is a great place for bargains and
crammed with shops selling handicrafts and souvenirs. Vendors may
offer to take you to 'secret rooms'
in the back of the building, which
are crammed with knock-off designer bags and watches. (Karama
Shopping Complex; www.facebook.
com/karamaMarketDubai; 18B St;
🕑10am-10pm; Ⓜ ADCB)

Dream Girl Tailors CLOTHING

39 🅐 MAP P56, E2

Kamal Makhija and his army of
tailors have had women looking
good since 1971. They can create
original designs, copy a beloved
dress or even sew you an outfit
from a magazine photo. A dress
will cost you around Dhs150,
depending on the complexity of
the pattern, a skirt around Dhs60.
(📞04 388 0070; www.dreamgirl
tailors.com; Al Futtaim Bldg, 37D St,
Meena Bazaar; 🕑10am-1pm & 4-10pm
Sat-Thu, 6-9pm Fri; Ⓜ Mashreq)

Hollywood Tailors CLOTHING

40 🅐 MAP P56, E2

In business since 1976 and highly
reliable, this outfit specialises in

exquisitely tailored men's suits and
has lots of fabrics to choose from.
Turn-around time ranges from
three days to one week. (📞04
352 8551; www.hollywooduae.com;
37D St, Meena Bazaar; 🕑9.30am-
1.30pm & 4-10pm Sat-Thu, 6-9pm Fri;
Ⓜ Mashreq)

The One HOMEWARES

41 🅐 MAP P56, C8

Nirvana for design-minded home
decorators, this airy showroom
unites funky, innovative and
top-quality items from dozens of
international manufacturers. Even
everyday items get a zany twist
here, like pearl-beaded pillows,
tiger-print wing-back chairs and
vintage-style pendant lamps.
(📞600 541 007; www.theone.com; 1st
fl, Wafi Mall; 🕑10am-10pm Sun-Thu, to
midnight Fri & Sat; Ⓜ Dubai Healthcare
City)

Royal Saffron SPICES

42 🅐 MAP P56, E2

This tiny shop tucked into the
quiet lanes of Al Fahidi Historic
District (p52) is a photogenic find.
It's crammed full of spices like
cloves, cardamom and cinnamon,
plus fragrant oils, dried fruits and
nuts, frankincense from Somalia
and Oman, henna hair dye – and
quirky salt and pepper sheikh and
sheikhas. (📞050 282 9565; Al Fahidi
Historic District, Al Fahidi St; 🕑9am-
9pm; Ⓜ Mashreq)

Explore ◉

Jumeirah & Around

Hemmed in by the turquoise waters of the Gulf, Jumeirah translates as 'the beautiful' and is practically synonymous with beaches. Its main drag is Jumeirah Rd, which runs straight as a ruler parallel to the Gulf from the La Mer waterfront village to the Burj Al Arab and is lined by boutiques, cafes and businesses catering mostly to a well-heeled local clientele. The most interesting stretch begins near the swan-white Jumeirah Mosque, which is open to non-Muslims on guided tours. The Etihad Museum is a cultural focal point around here, as is 2nd December St with its street art.

Jumeirah is dominated by low-rise apartment buildings and white-washed villas. Although an older part of town, it also flaunts pockets of urban cool in the form of such lifestyle malls as BoxPark, Galleria and the sprawling City Walk development that's especially popular with Emirati hipsters and families. Right on the Gulf, La Mer offers an enticing blend of beach fun, popular restaurants and a waterpark.

The Dubai Canal and artificial offshore islands and peninsulas have also significantly reshaped Jumeirah in recent years. Don't miss an evening stroll along the canal promenade to view the motion-operated waterfall set against the sparkling skyline.

Getting There & Around

Jumeirah is not directly served by metro. The closest stops are World Trade Centre, Emirates Tower, Financial Centre and Burj Khalifa/Dubai Mall, all on the Red Line. From here you'll need to catch a taxi to your final destination. Bus 8 and 88 travel the entire length of Jumeirah Rd down to the Burj Al Arab.

Neighbourhood Map on p72

Jumeirah Mosque (p74) CHECCO2/SHUTTERSTOCK ©

Jumeirah & Around

0   500 m
0   0.25 miles

For reviews see
- ⊙ Sights   p74
- ✖ Eating   p77
- ⊙ Drinking   p80
- ⌂ Shopping   p81

THE GULF

Jumeirah Rd

Wonder Bus Tours

75A

13 ✖ 7 ⊙ ⌂ 21
15 ✖

8A

59A

14D

75B

79   77B

32C

JUMEIRAH 2

26C

32C

28B   69B   65B

Al Wasl Rd

2D

Al Wasl Rd   27 22
26 ⌂ ⌂ ⌂

✖ 8

⌂
13th St   23

20 ⌂

75

79   81

57A

17 ⌂

Green   4 ⊙   6
Planet   3 ⊙ ⊙ Mattel Play! Town
Dubai
Walls

Umm Amara St

13th St

Al Safa St

83B

58A

Burj Khalifa/
Dubai Mall
Ⓜ
Interchange
No 1

Sheikh Zayed Rd

DOWNTOWN
DUBAI

E   F   G   H

1
5
Nikki
Beach
Dubai

2

19
18
16
Etihad
Museum
2
La Mer
1 Jumeirah
Mosque
3
24
Jumeirah Rd
14
15B 27B
2D
6C
11
25A
6B 21A
4A
2B
25
2A
6B
10A
24A
2nd December St
11
16A
10B
24B
7
11
17B
3A
43A
35A
14A
45A
10D
16C 41A
41A
39B
10C
16B
35
20A
25B
27B
24C
23
21B
2A
17A
Al Wasl Rd
2A
6A
9
8A
12
Al Hudhaiba Rd
15
20B
24D
JUMEIRAH 1
27A
2A
14
2C
2B
43A
6B
29
31
8B
12B
12A
16B
18B
20A
14B
18B
24A
12A
16A
24A
18A
Satwa
Roundabout
Dubai
Street
Museum
4
49
45
41
25
23
10
Al Satwa Rd
57A
2nd December St
SATWA
6B
19
8A
6C
Al Satwa Rd
10B
8C
17
14A
63
18A
21
19
18B
20A
12A
22A
5
20B
22A
22B
22B
28A
30A
11
32C
308
73B
308
5
World Trade
Centre
Zabeel
Roundabout
6
57A
15
11
19
Sheikh Zayed Rd
Emirates
Towers
17
2nd Zabeel Rd
Financial
Centre
2
37
7
FINANCIAL
CENTRE
21

E   F   G   H

Sights

Jumeirah Mosque
MOSQUE

1 MAP P72, G3

Snowy white and intricately detailed, Jumeirah is Dubai's most beautiful mosque and one of only a handful in the UAE that are open to non-Muslims – one-hour guided tours are operated by the Sheikh Mohammed Centre for Cultural Understanding (p58). Tours conclude with pastries and a discussion session during which you're free to ask any question about Islam and Emirati culture. There's no need to book. Modest dress is preferred, but traditional clothing can be borrowed for free. Cameras are allowed. (📞04 353 6666; www.cultures.ae; Jumeirah Rd, Jumeirah 1; tours Dhs20; ⏱tours 10am Sat-Thu; 🅿; MEmirates Towers, World Trade Centre)

Etihad Museum
MUSEUM

2 MAP P72, H3

This striking modern museum engagingly chronicles the birth of the UAE in 1971, spurred by the discovery of oil in the 1950s and the withdrawal of the British in 1968. Documentary films, photographs, artefacts, timelines and interactive displays zero in on historic milestones in the years leading up to and immediately following this momentous occasion and pay homage to the country's seven founding fathers. Free tours of the adjacent circular Union House, where the agreement was signed, are available. (📞04 515 5771; http://etihadmuseum.dubaiculture.ae; Jumeirah St, Jumeirah 1; adult/child Dhs25/10; ⏱10am-8pm; 🅿; MMax)

Dubai Walls
PUBLIC ART

3 MAP P72, C5

More than a dozen hot shots of the international street-art scene, including Aiko, Blek Le Rat, ROA and Nick Walker, have turned urban-style quarter City Walk into a stunning outdoor gallery. The not-to-be-missed art ranges from small pop-up model art to full-on installations covering an entire wall. The project was sponsored

Urban Art on 2nd December St

In 2016, 16 local and international street artists mounted their cherry-pickers to turn the rather drab facades on 2nd December St into the **Dubai Street Museum** (Map p72, H4; 2nd December St, Satwa; ⏱24hr; MMax), a striking outdoor gallery with murals reflecting Dubai's Bedouin heritage. Highlights include: *Emirati children* by French artist Seth Globepainter; *Resting Falcon* by Hua Tunan from China; *Founding Fathers* by Emirati artist Ashwaq Abdulla and *Old Man in Boat* by Russian artist Julia Volchkova.

PHOENIXPRODUCTION/SHUTTERSTOCK ©

Green Planet

by City Walk developer Meraas.
(City Walk, Jumeirah 1; ⏰24hr; Ⓜ Burj
Khalifa/Dubai Mall)

Green Planet ZOO

4 ◉ MAP P72, C5

If you can build a ski slope in the
desert, why not a rainforest too?
The Green Planet is an indoor
tropical paradise intended to
'edutain' about biodiversity, nature
and sustainability. More than 3000
animals and plants live beneath its
green canopy, including birds, butterflies, frogs, spiders and snakes.
The latest addition is a bat cave on
the 4th floor. The small fruit bats
can be hard to spot; if possible
visit at 2pm when they are fed.
(www.thegreenplanetdubai.com; City
Walk, Al Madina St, Jumeirah 1; adult/
child Dhs110/74; ⏰10am-6pm; Ⓟ 🚹;
Ⓜ Burj Khalifa/Dubai Mall)

Nikki Beach Dubai BEACH

5 ◉ MAP P72, H1

At this fashionable pleasure pit
on the emerging Pearl Jumeirah
residential peninsula, the crisp all-
white look sets the stage for some
serious partying. On weekends, the
bronzed, beautiful and cashed-
up descend on the Dubai branch
of the famous Miami beach club
to frolic in the vast pool, lounge
on daybeds, load up on seafood
and toast the sunset with bubbly.
Weekdays are quieter. (📞04 376
6162; www.nikkibeach.com/destin
ations/beach-clubs/dubai; Pearl Jumeirah Island, Jumeirah 1; sunloungers
with reservation weekdays/weekends

Creating Dubai Canal

Water was released into the Dubai Canal (also called Dubai Water Canal) on 1 November 2016, marking the culmination of an amazing feat of engineering that connects the mouth of Dubai Creek with the Gulf. The Creek's first 2.2km extension created the Business Bay district and was completed in 2007. In November 2016 construction was completed on the last 3.2km segment that cuts from Business Bay below Sheikh Zayed Rd and through Safa Park before spilling into the sea at Jumeirah Beach.

Office and hotel high-rises are being built at a frantic pace in Business Bay (including the edgy **Dubai Design District**), the waterfront is lined with residences, boutique hotels, cafes, marinas and other public spaces. A floating restaurant and yacht club are also planned, as well as other state-of-the-art waterborne buildings. A promenade conducive to jogging and walking parallels both banks. A highlight is the illuminated and motion-operated **waterfall** (p112) that cascades down both sides of Sheikh Zayed Bridge from 7pm to 10pm, stopping only for passing vessels. The **Dubai Ferry** runs several times daily from Al Jaddaf Marine Station at the mouth of Dubai Creek to Jumeirah.

Dhs150/300; 11am-9pm Sep-Jun; P; MMax)

Wed, to 10pm Thu, 10am-10pm Fri; ; MBurj Khalifa/Dubai Mall)

Mattel Play! Town PLAYGROUND

6 MAP P72, C5

In this adorable indoor playground, the milk-tooth brigade get to build a house with Bob the Builder, put out fires with Fireman Sam, dance in front of a magic mirror with Angelina Ballerina and hang out with Barney and Thomas the Tank Engine. Parents, meanwhile, have free admission and can nibble on a salad or lasagne at the cafe. (800 637 227; www.playtowndubai. com; City Walk, Jumeirah 2; 1hr/2hr/day Dhs59/89/99; 9am-8pm Sat-

Wonder Bus Tours BOATING

7 MAP P72, C3

These unusual sightseeing tours have you boarding the bright yellow amphibious Wonder Bus at the Mercato Shopping Mall, driving down to Dubai Creek, plunging into the water, cruising past historic Bur Dubai and Deira and returning to the mall, all within the space of an hour. Tours run several times daily. (04 359 5656, 050 181 0553; www.wonderbusdubai.net; Mercato Shopping Mall, Jumeirah Rd, Jumeirah 1; adult/child 3-11yr Dhs155/135; MBurJuman)

Eating

Logma
EMIRATI $$

8 MAP P72, B4

This funky Emirati cafe is a great introduction to contemporary local cuisine. It's popular for breakfast dishes such as shakshuka (poached eggs in a spicy tomato sauce topped with feta), wholesome salads (try the pomegranate mozzarella) and sandwiches made with traditional *khameer* bread. Swap your usual latte for sweet *karak chai* (spiced tea) – a local obsession – or a date shake. (800 56462; www.logma.ae; BoxPark, Al Wasl Rd, Jumeirah 1; mains Dhs44-65; 8am-1am; 12, 15, 93, Business Bay)

3 Fils
ASIAN $$

9 MAP P72, B3

Singaporean chef Akmal Anuar turns out innovative yet unpretentious Asian-influenced small plates at this tiny, unlicensed spot – a perfect foil to Dubai's expensive, overblown eateries. There are around 25 seats inside and a pint-sized kitchen in the corner, but try to nab one of the outside tables overlooking the bobbing yachts in the marina. Reservations are not taken. (056 273 0030; www.3fils.com; Jumeirah Fishing Harbour, Al Urouba St, Jumeirah 1; sharing plates Dhs38-75; 1-11pm Mon-Wed, to midnight Thu-Sat; Burj Khalifa/Dubai Mall)

Ravi
PAKISTANI $

10 MAP P72, H4

Since 1978, everyone from cabbies to professional chefs has flocked to this Pakistani eatery, where you eat like a prince and pay like a pauper. Loosen your belt for heaped portions of grilled meats or succulent curries, including a few meatless options. Service is swift if perfunctory. Near the Satwa Roundabout. Cash only.

Standouts include the daal fry and chicken tikka. (04 331 5353; Al Satwa Rd, Satwa; mains Dhs8-25; 5am-2.30am; ; World Trade Centre)

Lime Tree Cafe
CAFE $

11 MAP P72, G3

This comfy Euro-style cafe is an expat favourite famous for its luscious cakes (especially the carrot cake), tasty breakfasts,

Vive La Mer

With shops, restaurants, a beachfront with hammocks and a huge playpark, **La Mer** (p79) is Dubai's newest beachfront destination and it's free to sunbathe or roam the complex. Kids will love the inflatable playground, and you're spoiled for choice when it comes to eating – try Motomachi for Japanese desserts or go local at Treej Cafe.

Call to Prayer

While staying near a mosque, you'll most likely be woken up around 4.30am by the inimitable wailing of the *azan* (the Muslim call to prayer). There's a haunting beauty to the sound, one that you'll only hear in Islamic countries. Muslims pray five times a day: at dawn; when the sun is directly overhead; when the sun is in the position that creates shadows the same length as the object shadowed; at the beginning of sunset; and at twilight, when the last light of the sun disappears over the horizon.

The exact times are printed in the daily newspapers and on websites. Muslims needn't be near a mosque to pray; they need only face Mecca. Those who cannot get to a mosque, may stop and pray wherever they are.

creative sandwiches (stuffed into its homemade Turkish pide), roast chicken and pastas. It's located next to Spinneys supermarket. (📞04 325 6325; www.thelimetreecafe. com; Jumeirah Rd, Jumeirah 1; mains Dhs24-40; ⏰7.30am-6pm; 🛜🚫; Ⓜ World Trade Centre)

Al Mallah   MIDDLE EASTERN $

12 ✖ MAP P72, H4

Locals praise the chicken sha-warma and grilled chicken at this traditional joint (which started life as a juice bar some 30 years ago). It is located on one of Dubai's most pleasant, liveliest and oldest walking streets with shaded outdoor seating. If nothing else, sample its fresh mango or papaya juice. (📞04 398 4723; 2nd December St, Satwa; sandwiches Dhs7-15; ⏰6am-2.30am; Ⓜ Max)

Al Fanar   EMIRATI $$

13 ✖ MAP P72, C3

Al Fanar lays on the old-timey Emirati theme pretty thick with a Land Rover parked outside, a reed ceiling and waiters dressed in traditional garb. Give your taste buds a workout with such local classics as *machboos* (spicy casserole with rice), *saloona* (tomato-based stew) or *harees* (a porridge-like dish with meat). Breakfast is served all day. (📞04 344 2141; www.alfanar restaurant.com; 1st fl, Town Center Mall, Jumeirah Rd, Jumeirah 1; mains Dhs42-95; ⏰noon-9.30pm Sun-Wed, to 10pm Thu, 9am-10pm Fri, to 9.30pm Sat; Ⓜ Burj Khalifa/Dubai Mall)

Comptoir 102   HEALTH FOOD $$

14 ✖ MAP P72, E3

In a pretty cottage with a quiet patio out the back, this concept cafe comes attached to a boutique selling beautiful things for home and hearth. The daily changing menu rides the local-organic-seasonal wave and eschews gluten, sugar and dairy. There's also a big selection of vitamin-packed juices, smoothies and desserts. It's opposite Beach Centre mall. (📞04 385 4555; www.comptoir102.com; 102 Jumeirah Rd, Jumeirah 1; mains Dhs50-65, 3-course meal Dhs90; ⏰7.30am-9pm; 🛜📶; Ⓜ Emirates Towers)

Kaak Al Manara   LEBANESE $

15 🍴 MAP P72, D3

Kaak is flat sesame bread that's a street-food staple in Lebanon. This upbeat mall-based eatery serves it with various sweet and savoury fillings, sprinkled with *zaatar* (a blend of spices that includes hyssop and sesame) or sumac, and toasted just right. Try the classic picon cheese spread or a fusion special like the chicken fajita *kaak*. (📞04 258 2003; https://kaak-al-manara. business.site; 1st fl, Mercato Shopping Mall, Jumeirah Rd, Jumeirah 1; dishes Dhs18-32; ⏰8.30am-midnight Sat-Wed, to 1am Thu & Fri; 🅿📶; Ⓜ Burj Khalifa/Dubai Mall)

Salt   BURGERS $

16 🍴 MAP P72, F3

Salt started life as a roaming food truck serving delicious mini-burgers, before graduating to a silver Airstream parked permanently at **La Mer** (Map p72, F3; 📞800 637 227; www.lamerdubai. ae; Jumeirah 1; ⏰10am-midnight; 🅿). Join the ever-present queue to place your order and then pull up some pallet furniture set right on the sand (or inside the

Etihad Museum (p74)

CREATIVEHYMMS/SHUTTERSTOCK ©

Mercato Shopping Mall

air-conditioned glass cube, if the sun is starting to bite).

The tiny menu features just three types of sliders with grilled Wagyu beef or deep-fried chicken – the latter is topped with Cheetos, a nod to the locals' love of crushed crisps, cheese and hot sauce. Add a side order of fries and a calorific Lotus milkshake made with sweetly spiced Belgian biscuits. (www.find-salt.com; La Mer; sliders Dhs30-50; ◷9am-3am; 🛜; Ⓜ Al Safa)

Drinking

Grapeskin   WINE BAR

17 ⓟ MAP P72, C5

At this stylish rustic wine bar imbued with a homey vibe, you can match your wine to your mood. Most pours come from small vineyards and are served with fine cheeses, cold cuts and sharing platters. Chill with shisha on the terrace or join the post-work expat crowd for happy hour between 6pm and 8pm. (📞 04 403 3111; www.livelaville.com/dining/Grapeskin; La Ville Hotel & Suites, City Walk, Al Multaqa St, Jumeirah 1; ◷4pm-1am Sun-Thu; to 2am Fri & Sat; 🛜; Ⓜ Burj Khalifa/Dubai Mall)

Club Boudoir   CLUB

18 ⓟ MAP P72, G2

High on the glam-o-meter, Boudoir has been around the block once or twice but still pulls in beautiful punters with nights dedicated to hip-hop and R&B and others to *desi* (Bollywood music). (📞 04 345 5995; www.clubboudoirdubai.com;

Dubai Marine Beach Resort & Spa, Jumeirah Rd, Jumeirah 1; ⏰10pm-3am; 📶; Ⓜ World Trade Centre)

Sho Cho BAR

19 🔵 MAP P72, G2

Although Sho Cho is primarily a Japanese restaurant, it's the heady lure of the cool Gulf breezes and potent cocktails on the laid-back terrace that continue to make this scene staple simply irresistible. (📞04 346 1111; www.sho-cho.com; Dubai Marine Beach Resort & Spa, Jumeirah Rd, Jumeirah 1; ⏰7pm-3am Sun-Fri; 📶; Ⓜ World Trade Centre, Emirates Towers)

Shopping

City Walk SHOPPING CENTRE

20 🔒 MAP P72, C4

This city-centre shopping, dining and entertainment district has the feel of a European town centre with its faux Georgian-style buildings, water features and pavements lined with trees. Along with an ever-increasing number of shops, cafes and restaurants, there is a 10-screen cinema complex and a handful of family-friendly attractions. (www.citywalk.ae; Al Safa Rd, Jumeirah 2; ⏰10am-10pm; 📶; Ⓜ Burj Khalifa/Dubai Mall)

Mercato Shopping Mall SHOPPING CENTRE

21 🔒 MAP P72, D3

With 140 stores, Mercato may be small by Dubai standards, but it's

distinguished by attractive architecture that looks like a fantasy blend of a classic train station and an Italian Renaissance town. Think vaulted glass roof, brick arches, a giant clock and a cafe-lined piazza. Retail-wise, you'll find upscale international brands and a Spinneys supermarket. (📞04 344 4161; www.mercato shoppingmall.com; Jumeirah Rd, Jumeirah 1; ⏰10am-10pm; Ⓜ Financial Centre, Burj Khalifa/Dubai Mall)

BoxPark SHOPPING CENTRE

22 🔒 MAP P72, A4

Inspired by the London original, this 1.3km-long outdoor lifestyle mall was built from upcycled shipping containers and has injected a welcome dose of urban cool into the Dubai shopping scene. The 220 units draw a hip crowd, including lots of locals, with quirky concept stores, eclectic cafes and restaurants, and entertainment options including a cinema with on-demand screenings. (📞800 637 227; www.boxpark.ae; Al Wasl Rd, Jumeirah 2; ⏰10am-midnight; 📶; Ⓜ Business Bay)

Galleria Mall SHOPPING CENTRE

23 🔒 MAP P72, B4

The modern-Middle Eastern design of this locally adored boutique mall is as much a draw as the shops, which include rare gems like the first UAE branch of Saudi homeware store Cities, and Blossom and Bloom, selling raw organic honey from around the world. Wrap up a visit with a healthy lunch at South African cafe Tashas or gooey cakes from Emirati-owned Home Bakery. (📞04 344 4434; www.galleria-mall.ae; Al Wasl Rd, Jumeirah 2; 🕙10am-midnight; Ⓜ Burj Khalifa/Dubai Mall)

S*uce
FASHION & ACCESSORIES

24 🔒 MAP P72, F3

Plain and simple they are not, the clothes and accessories at S*uce (pronounced 'sauce'), a pioneer in Dubai's growing lifestyle-fashion scene. Join fashionistas picking through regional and international designers and brands you probably won't find on your high street back home, including Alice McCall, Bleach and Fillyboo.

This is the original store. There are others in Dubai Mall, at The Beach at JBR and in the Galleria Mall. (📞04 344 7270; www.shopatsauce.com; ground fl, Village Mall, Jumeirah Rd, Jumeirah 1; 🕙10am-10pm Sat-Thu, from 4pm Fri; Ⓜ Emirates Towers)

O Concept
FASHION & ACCESSORIES

25 🔒 MAP P72, G3

This Emirati-owned urban boutique-cafe with shiny concrete floors and ducts wrapped in gold foil is a routine stop for fashionistas in search of up-to-the-second T-shirts, dresses, jeans and other casual-elegant fashions and accessories.

The cafe has delicious cappuccino and gluten-, sugar- and dairy-free desserts that actually taste good. (📞04 345 5557; www.facebook.com/Oconceptstore; Al Hudheiba

Roxy Cinemas, BoxPark (p81)

Buying Alcohol in Dubai

One of the most common questions among first-time visitors is: 'Can I drink alcohol in Dubai?' The answer is yes – in some places.

Tourists over 21 are allowed to drink alcohol in designated areas such as licensed bars and clubs attached to Western-style hotels. By law, drinking anywhere else does require being in possession of an alcohol licence; which is only issued to non-Muslim residents. The licence grants the right to purchase a fixed monthly limit of alcohol sold in special liquor stores such as African & Eastern and in some branches of Spinneys supermarket. Note that visitors are not officially permitted to purchase alcohol in these places, and staff are supposed to ask to see the licence.

When arriving by air, non-Muslim visitors over 18 may buy 4L of spirits, wine or beer in the airport duty-free shop. However, it is illegal to transport alcohol without a licence, whether in a taxi, hire car or the Dubai Metro. In practice, this is widely ignored.

Rd, Jumeirah 1; 10am-10pm; ; World Trade Centre)

Urbanist HOMEWARES

26 MAP P72, A4

The Syrian couple behind Urbanist dedicate the shop's shelf space to hand-curated items rooted in both tradition and modernity, and Western and Middle Eastern tastes. None of the pieces – from tiny gold earrings to tunics and fez-shaped stools – are run of the mill. It's all displayed in a vibrant space where industrial cool meets antique cabinets and mother-of-pearl mirrors. (04 348 8002; www.facebook.com/Urbaniststore; BoxPark, Al Wasl Rd, Jumeirah 2; 10am-10pm Sun-Thu, to midnight Fri & Sat; Business Bay)

Typo STATIONERY

27 MAP P72, A4

This is the kind of shop where 'notebooks' are still made from paper. Indeed, here they come in all shapes and sizes, from cutesy to corporate, along with lots of other fun but useful items like laptop bags, pencil cases and mobile phone covers.

There are several other branches around town, including Dubai Mall and City Centre Deira. (04 385 6631; http://typo.com; BoxPark, Al Wasl Rd, Jumeirah 2; 10am-10pm Sun-Wed, to midnight Thu & Fri; Business Bay)

Explore ⊕

Burj Al Arab & Madinat Jumeirah

The iconic Burj Al Arab is the shining star of this beautiful stretch of coast, also home to Madinat Jumeirah, a canal-laced 'Arabian Venice' complete with hotels, cafes and boutiques. Away from the resorts, Kite and Sunset beaches are fabulous public ribbons of sand, while inland, fun shopping awaits at the Mall of the Emirates, which also shelters the deliciously surreal Ski Dubai indoor ski park.

If you're in town for a beach holiday, you could hardly find a finer stretch of sandy delight than around the Burj Al Arab, the famous superluxe resort that's the iconic symbol of Dubai's boom years. But even if you're not staying in a fancy Gulf-adjacent hotel, you can frolic on public beaches offering everything from water-sports rentals to global street-food treats. One stretch is even open at night for floodlit swims.

Want to shop in the souq but don't care for the dust, hubbub and haggling? At Souq Madinat Jumeirah you can bask in air-conditioned refinement while still soaking up Arabian Nights flair in its warren of narrow walkways shaded by carved wooden roofs. If you're more into mall-style shopping, head inland to the Mall of the Emirates to pick out some chic new threads.

Getting There & Around

The closest Metro stop to the Burj Al Arab, Madinat Jumeirah and Sunset Beach is Mall of the Emirates on the Red Line. For Kite Beach, get off at Al Safa. You'll still need to catch a taxi to reach your final destination.

Neighbourhood Map on p92

Top Experience

Step into a Modern Souq at Madinat Jumeirah

One of Dubai's most attractive modern developments, this resort is a contemporary version of a traditional Arab village, complete with a souq, palm-fringed waterways and desert-coloured hotels and villas festooned with wind towers. At its heart lies souk Madinat Jumeirah, a mazelike bazaar with shops lining wood-framed walkways and canalside restaurants.

◉ MAP P92, C3

☏ 04 366 8888

www.jumeirah.com

King Salman Bin Abdulaziz Al Saud St, Umm Suqeim 3

Ⓜ Mall of the Emirates

Souk Madinat Jumeirah

Although the ambience at this maze-like **bazaar** (pictured; Madinat Jumeirah; 10am-11pm;) is too contrived to feel like an authentic Arabian market, the quality of some of the crafts, art and souvenirs is actually quite high. There are numerous cafes, bars and restaurant, the nicest of which overlook the waterways and the Burj Al Arab.

Abra Cruising

The desert seems far away as you glide past enchanting gardens of billowing bougainvillea, bushy banana trees and soaring palms on a 20-minute **cruise** (Souk Madinat Jumeirah; adult/child Dhs85/50; 10am-11pm Nov-Apr, from 11am May-Oct) aboard a traditional-style abra (wooden boat). Tours leave from the Souk Madinat waterfront. No reservations are necessary.

Turtle Watching

The nonprofit **Dubai Turtle Rehabilitation Project** (www.facebook.com/turtle. rehabilitation) at the Jumeirah Al Naseem resort has nursed more than 560 injured or sick sea turtles back to health and released them into the Gulf. The turtles spend the last weeks before their release in the hotel's sea-fed lagoon, which can be visited daily. Feedings take place at 11am on Wednesdays.

Saturday Brunch

Saturday brunch is a time-honoured tradition, especially among Western expats. The Madinat hotels Al Qasr and Mina A'Salam are both famous for putting on a mindboggling cornucopia of delectables – from roast lamb and sushi to cooked-to-order seafood and beautiful salads.

★ Top Tips

o If you are staying at a Madinat hotel or eating at one of the restaurants, your abra shuttle is free.

o Make dinner or brunch reservations at least one week ahead for most of the restaurants.

o Take advantage of happy-hour deals offered at many Madinat bars.

o Maps are available at several information points.

✗ Take a Break

For sunset drinks with a view of the Burj Al Arab, the rug-lined terrace of the Bahri Bar (p97) is a perfect vantage point.

Book early for delicious seafood with Madinat and Burj Al Arab views at chic and sophisticated Pierchic (p96).

Burj Al Arab & Madinat Jumeirah Madinat Jumeirah

Top Experience 📷
Sip Cocktails at Burj Al Arab

When Dubai's ruler commissioned the Burj Al Arab in the 1990s, he gave architect Tom Wright a blank cheque to dream up an iconic structure that the entire world would associate with the tiny Gulf emirate. The final tally came to $1.5 billion, but the gamble paid off: the Burj Al Arab's graceful silhouette, inspired by the billowing sail of a dhow, is as iconic to Dubai as the Eiffel Tower is to Paris.

◎ MAP P92, D2

📞 04 301 7777

www.jumeirah.com

off Jumeirah Rd, Umm Suqeim 3

Ⓜ Mall of the Emirates

Architecture & Design

The Burj has 60 floors spread over 321m and was the world's tallest hotel at the time of its opening. British architect Tom Wright came up with the iconic design and signature translucent fibreglass facade that serves as a shield from the desert sun during the day and as a screen for the impressive illumination at night.

Interior

The Burj interior by British-Chinese designer Khuan Chew is every bit as over-the-top as the exterior is simple and elegant. The moment you step into the lofty lobby, a crescendo of gold-leaf, crystal chandeliers, hand-knotted carpets, water elements, pillars and other design elements put you into sensory overload. Some of the 24,000 sq metres of marble hail from the same quarry where Michelangelo got his material.

Optical Effect

The white metal crosspieces at the top of the Burj Al Arab form what is said to be the largest cross in the Middle East – but it's only visible from the sea. By the time this unexpected feature was discovered, it was too late to redesign the tower – the hotel had already put Dubai on the map and become the icon for the city. See the cross on a boat charter and decide for yourself. The scale is amazing.

Tea with a View

A cocktail or afternoon tea in this capsule-shaped **Skyview Bar** (04 301 7600; www.burjalarab.com; 1pm-2am Sat-Thu, from 7pm Fri) sticking out from the main building on the 27th floor is high on the to-do list of many Dubai visitors despite the steep minimum spends. Reservations are essential.

★ Top Tips

o If you're not checking into the Burj, you need to make a reservation for cocktails, afternoon tea or a meal to get past lobby security (a minimum spend applies; the website has details).

o For a surreal dining experience, book a table at Al Mahara (p96) to nosh on fish and seafood while seated before a giant, round aquarium.

✗ Take a Break

For romantic views of the Burj, head to the bars in Madinat Jumeirah, such as Folly by Nick & Scott (p98).

Walking Tour 🚶

Gallery Hopping Around Alserkal Avenue

*The most cutting-edge galleries within Dubai's growing art scene cluster in a sprawling warehouse campus called **Alserkal Avenue** (www.alserkal avenue.ae; 17th St, Al Quoz 1; M Al Safa, Umm Al Seef) in an industrial area called Al Quoz, east of Sheikh Zayed Rd. It's the brainchild of developer and arts patron Abdelmonem bin Eisa Alserkal.*

Walk Facts

Start Tom & Serg

End Ayyam Gallery

Length 3km; as long as you like to admire the galleries

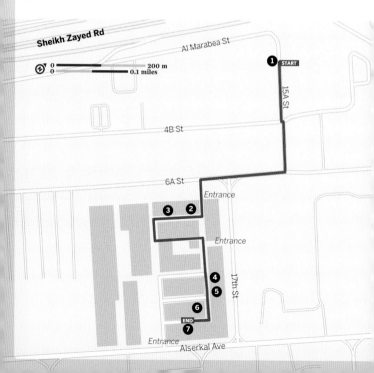

❶ Tom & Serg

Fuel up for your gallery hop at this lofty warehouse-style **cafe** (www.tomandserg.com; Al Joud Center, 15A St, Al Quoz 1; ⏲8am-4pm Sun-Thu, to 6pm Fri & Sat; 📶🖊) with concrete floors, exposed pipes and an open kitchen. The menu teems with feel-good food such as Moroccan chicken, eggs Benedict and a mean burger on a homemade bun.

❷ The Third Line

This **gallery** (www.thethirdline.com; 78-80 Alserkal Ave, Al Quoz 1; ⏲10am-7pm Sat-Thu) has been a cornerstone of Dubai's growing gallery scene since 2005. It frequently introduces Emirati artists to collectors and art aficionados at such prestigious fairs as Art Basel.

❸ Mirzam Chocolate Makers

Mirzam (www.mirzam.com; Warehouse 70, Alserkal Ave, Al Quoz 1; ⏲10am-7pm Sat-Thu; 🚶) operates a chocolate factory where visitors can watch all stages of production – from roasting to hand-wrapping – taking place in a glass-encased chocolate laboratory. Drop by the integrated shop to sample and buy the final product. Staff host one-hour tour and tasting workshops (Dhs37), plus classes for children. Sign up via the website.

❹ Leila Heller Gallery

For over three decades, this prestigious New York **gallery** (www.leilahellergallery.com; 86-87 Alserkal Ave, Al Quoz 1; ⏲10am-7pm Sat-Thu) has been a conduit for artistic and cultural dialogue between Western, Middle Eastern, Central Asian and Southeast Asian artists. Artists on its roster range include Tony Cragg and Pakistani artist Rashid Rana.

❺ Fridge

This talent management **agency** (www.thefridgedubai.com; 5 Alserkal Ave, Al Quoz 1; tickets from Dhs50) runs a much-beloved concert series (usually on Fridays) that shines the spotlight on local talent still operating below the radar.

❻ Gallery Isabelle van den Eynde

This edgy **gallery** (www.ivde.net; 17 Alserkal Ave, Al Quoz 1; ⏲10am-7pm Sat-Thu) has been a household name on the Dubai art scene since 2006. It promotes progressive and emerging talent from around the region and often presents envelope-pushing exhibits. Artists represented include Hassan Sharif and Bita Fayyazi.

❼ Ayyam Gallery

This top **gallery's** (www.ayyamgallery.com; B11 Alserkal Ave, Al Quoz 1) main mission is to promote emerging Middle Eastern (especially Syrian) artists and to introduce their often provocative, political and feminist work and voices to a wider audience.

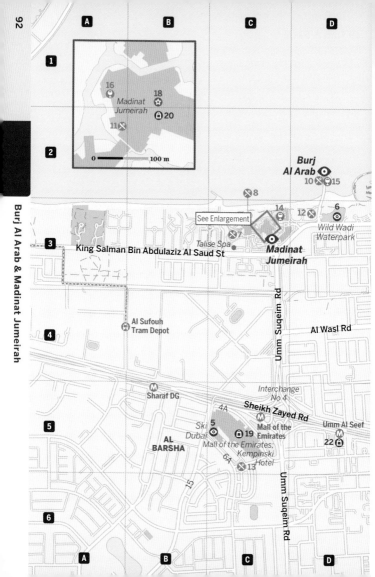

A   **B**   **C**   **D**

1

16

18

Madinat Jumeirah

20

11

2

0   100 m

Burj Al Arab

10   15

8

14   12   6

See Enlargement

Talise Spa

7

Wild Wadi Waterpark

Madinat Jumeirah

3

King Salman Bin Abdulaziz Al Saud St

Umm Suqeim Rd

4

Al Sufouh Tram Depot

Al Wasl Rd

Sharaf DG

Interchange No 4

Sheikh Zayed Rd

4A

5

Ski Dubai

5

19   Mall of the Emirates

Umm Al Seef

22

AL BARSHA

Mall of the Emirates; Kempinski Hotel

6A

13

Umm Suqeim Rd

15

6

A   **B**   **C**   **D**

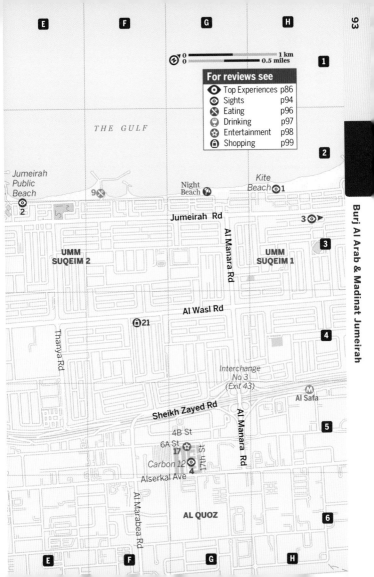

E　F　G　H

1

⊘ 0 ———————— 1 km
　0 ———————— 0.5 miles

For reviews see	
◉ Top Experiences	p86
◉ Sights	p94
✖ Eating	p96
🍷 Drinking	p97
★ Entertainment	p98
🛍 Shopping	p99

2

THE GULF

Jumeirah
Public
Beach
◉
2

9✖

Night
Beach ⚑

Kite
Beach ◉1

3 ◉▶

Jumeirah Rd

3

UMM
SUQEIM 2

UMM
SUQEIM 1

Al Manara Rd

Al Wasl Rd

4

🛍21

Thanya Rd

Interchange
No 3
(Exit 43)

Ⓜ
Al Safa

Sheikh Zayed Rd

Al Manara Rd

5

4B St

6A St

17th St

17 ★

Carbon 12 ◉
4

Alserkal Ave

Al Marabea Rd

AL QUOZ

6

E　F　G　H

Sights

Kite Beach
BEACH

1 MAP P92, H2

This long, pristine stretch of white sand, off Jumeirah Rd and next to a mosque, is superclean and has lots of activities, including kitesurfing, beach tennis, beach volleyball and kayaking. There are showers, wi-fi, toilets and changing facilities, plus lots of food trucks and cafes. Great views of the Burj Al Arab. (Sheikh Hamdan Beach; 2c St, off Jumeirah Rd, behind Saga World mall, Umm Suqeim 1; ⏲sunrise-sunset; Ⓜ Al Safa)

Jumeirah Public Beach
BEACH

2 ⊙ MAP P92, E3

Just north of the Jumeirah Beach Hotel, this public beach (also known as Sunset Beach) is perfect for snapping that envy-inducing

---

Night Swimming

Fancy a night-time swim with the twinkling Burj Al Arab as a backdrop? You can legally take a post-sunset dip along a 125m stretch of **beach** (Map p92, G2; Umm Suqeim 1 Beach; ⏲sunset-midnight; Ⓜ Umm Al Seef) illuminated by 12m-high wind- and solar-powered floodlights ('Smart Power Poles') and staffed with lifeguards. Find it about 1km north of the iconic landmark.

---

selfie with the Burj Al Arab as a backdrop. The wide, sandy strip has great infrastructure, including toilets, showers, changing cubicles and wi-fi via Smart Palms.

Jumeirah Public Beach is also Dubai's last surfing beach, with small to medium waves that are perfect for beginners. It's backed by tranquil Umm Suqeim Park. (Umm Suqeim Beach; Umm Suqeim 3; ; Ⓜ Umm Al Seef, Mall of the Emirates)

Majlis Ghorfat Um Al Sheef
HISTORIC BUILDING

3 ⊙ MAP P92, H3

This rare vestige of pre-oil times was built in 1955 as the summer retreat of Sheikh Rashid Bin Saeed Al Maktoum, the father of current ruler Sheikh Mohammed. The traditional two-storey gypsum-and-coral structure sports a palm-frond roof, a wind tower and window shutters carved from East African timber. The rug-lined *majlis* (reception room) offers a glimpse into royal leisure living. The palm garden features a traditional *falaj* irrigation system. (☏ 04 226 0286; near Al Mehemal & Al Bagaara Sts, Jumeirah 3; adult/child Dhs3/1; ⏲7.30am-2.30pm Sun-Thu; Ⓜ Business Bay, Al Safa)

Carbon 12
GALLERY

4 ⊙ MAP P92, G5

This minimalist white-cube space serves as a gateway to the UAE art scene for accomplished artists from around the world, and vice-versa. Some of them have

VIVEK BR/SHUTTERSTOCK ©

Jumeirah Public Beach

roots in the Middle East, such as Tehran-born New York resident Sara Rahbar. (☑04 340 6016; www.carbon12dubai.com; 37 Alserkal Ave, Al Quoz 1; ⏰11.30am-7pm Sat-Thu; Ⓜ Al Safa, Umm Al Seef)

Ski Dubai
SKIING

5 ⊙ MAP P92, C5

Picture this: it's 45°C outside, and you're wearing gloves and a hat and riding a chairlift through a faux alpine winter wonderland. Skiing in the desert? No problem. In Dubai, that is. Ski Dubai has delighted everyone from slope-starved expats to curious tourists and snow virgins since opening in 2005 as the first indoor ski park in the Middle East. (☑toll free 800 386; www.skidxb.com; Mall of the Emirates, Sheikh Zayed Rd, Al Barsha; slope day pass adult/child Dhs310/285, snow park Dhs210; ⏰10am-11pm Mon-Thu, to midnight Fri, 9am-midnight Sat & Sun; ; Ⓜ Mall of the Emirates)

Wild Wadi Waterpark
WATER PARK

6 ⊙ MAP P92, D3

It's liquid thrills galore at Wild Wadi, where you can ride a water roller coaster (Master Blaster), plunge down a death-defying tandem slide (Jumeirah Sceirah) and get tossed around watery tornadoes (Tantrum Alley). Mellow types can chill on the lazy river, while kids love romping around a vast water playground with smaller slides and a dumping bucket. (☑04 348 4444; www.wildwadi.com; Jumeirah Rd, Jumeirah 3; over/under 110cm tall Dhs336/284;

Yoga on the Beach

Downward dog and sun salutation with a view of the Burj Al Arab? Just sign up for the daily sunset yoga sessions (Dhs90) organised by the on-site **Talise Spa** (Map p92, C3; 📞04 366 6818; www.jumeirah.com; Al Qasr Hotel, Madinat Jumeirah, Umm Suqeim 3; 🕑9am-10pm; Ⓜ Mall of the Emirates) and on Madinat Jumeirah's private beach. An even more spiritual journey awaits during Full Moon Yoga (Dhs99) – if you can get the timing right.

🕑10am-6pm Nov-Feb, to 7pm Mar-Oct; 🚻; Ⓜ Mall of the Emirates)

Eating

Pai Thai   THAI $$$

7 ❌ MAP P92, C3

An abra ride, a canalside table and candlelight are the hallmarks of a romantic night out, and this enchanting spot sparks on all cylinders. If your date doesn't make you swoon, then such expertly seasoned Thai dishes as wok-fried seafood and steamed sea bass should still ensure an unforgettable evening. Early reservations advised. (📞04 432 3232; www.jumeirah.com; Madinat Jumeirah, King Salman Bin Abdulaziz Al Saud St, Umm Suqeim 3; mains Dhs55-175; 🕑12.30-2.15pm & 6-11.15pm; 🛜; Ⓜ Mall of the Emirates)

Pierchic   SEAFOOD $$$

8 ❌ MAP P92, C2

Looking for a place to drop an engagement ring into a glass of champagne? Make reservations (far in advance) at this impossibly romantic seafood house with front-row views of the Burj Al Arab and Madinat Jumeirah. The menu is a foodie's dream, with a plethora of beautifully prepared dishes, including grilled Canadian lobster, a sheer crustacean delight. (📞04 432 3232; www.jumeirah.com; Madinat Jumeirah, King Salman Bin Abdulaziz Al Saud St, Umm Suqeim 3; mains Dhs125-450; 🕑1-2.30pm daily, plus 6.30-10pm Sun-Thu, to 10.30pm Fri & Sat; 🛜; Ⓜ Mall of the Emirates)

Bu Qtair   SEAFOOD $$

9 ❌ MAP P92, F2

Always packed to the gills, this simple eatery is a Dubai institution famous for its dock-fresh fish and shrimp, marinated in a 'secret' masala curry sauce and fried to order. Belly up to the window, point to what you'd like and wait for your order to be delivered to your table. Meals are priced by weight. (📞055 705 2130; off 2b St, Umm Suqeim Fishing Harbour, Umm Suqeim 1; meals Dhs40-125; 🕑noon-11.30pm; 🅿; Ⓜ Al Safa, Umm Al Seef)

Al Mahara   SEAFOOD $$$

10 ❌ MAP P92, D2

A lift posing as a submarine drops you into a gold-leaf-clad tunnel spilling into one of Dubai's most extravagant restaurants. Tables orbit a circular floor-to-ceiling aquarium where clownfish flit and baby sharks dart as their turbot and monkfish cousins are being devoured. Only the finest seafood imported from the UK – and prepared with deft simplicity – makes it onto plates here. A dress code is enforced, and no children under 12 for dinner. (☎04 301 7600; www.jumeirah.com; 1st fl, Burj Al Arab, Umm Suqeim 3; mains Dhs240-500, tasting menu Dhs995; ⏰12.30-3.30pm & 7-11.30pm; 🅿🛜)

Meat Co
STEAK $$$

11 ❌ MAP P92, A2

Surrender helplessly to your inner carnivore at this canalside meat temple where yummy cuts of aged steaks range from Australian grain-fed Angus to New Zealand grass-fed beast, all available in small (200g) and large (300g) portions. Book ahead for a canalside table with Burj Al Arab view or hide out from those vegetarian friends of yours in the dark-wood dining room. (☎04 368 6040; www.themeatco.com; Souq Madinat Jumeirah, King Salman Bin Abdulaziz Al Saud St, Umm Suqeim 3; mains Dhs165-390; ⏰noon-11.30pm Sun-Wed, to midnight Thu-Sat; 🅿🛜; Ⓜ Mall of the Emirates)

Rockfish
SEAFOOD $$$

12 ❌ MAP P92, D3

With silver-and-white interiors and a sandy terrace with front-row views of Burj Al Arab, Rockfish

serves up Mediterranean-style seafood in glam but unstuffy surroundings. The compact menu kicks off with crudo (raw seafood), moves on to salads and soups, and reaches a crescendo with piscine treats laced with Middle Eastern influences, like tiger prawns with pomegranate and coriander. (☎04 366 7640; www.jumeirah.com; Jumeirah Al Naseem, King Salman Bin Abdulaziz Al Saud St, Umm Suqeim 3; mains Dhs65-175; ⏰8-11am, 12.30-3.30pm & 6.30-11.30pm; 🅿🛜; 🚌81, Ⓜ Mall of the Emirates)

Al Amoor Express
EGYPTIAN $

13 ❌ MAP P92, C5

Vintage black-and-white photos of Egyptian actors keep an eye on diners here for their kushari fix (a mix of noodles, rice, black lentils, fried onions and tomato sauce), although it's more fun to order one of its famous cheese-, vegetable- or meat-stuffed fiteer pies and watch the baker sling and whirl the dough behind the counter.

The falafel also gets our thumbs up. (☎04 347 0787; Halim St, Al Barsha; mains Dhs10-56; ⏰7.30am-2am; Ⓜ Mall of the Emirates)

Drinking

Bahri Bar
BAR

14 🍸 MAP P92, C3

This chic bar drips with sultry Middle Eastern decor and has a veranda laid with Persian rugs and comfy sofas perfect for taking in magical views of the Madinat waterways and the Burj Al Arab. Daily drink deals, elevated bar bites, and bands or DJs playing jazz and soul make the place a perennial fave among locals and visitors. (📞04 432 3232; www.jumeirah. com; Mina A'Salam, Madinat Jumeirah, King Salman Bin Abdulaziz Al Saud St, Umm Suqeim 3; ⏱5pm-1am Mon-Fri, from 4pm Sat & Sun; 📶; Ⓜ Mall of the Emirates)

Gold on 27 COCKTAIL BAR

15 Ⓜ MAP P92, D2

Signature cocktails at this gold-dipped bar on the 27th floor of the Burj Al Arab are crafted with local lore or landmarks in mind and often feature surprise ingredients. The whisky-based Light Sweet Crude, for instance, also contains a smidgen of foie gras and charcoal-

Camel Company

infused truffle oil. Prices are as sky-high as the location, and reservations are essential. (📞04 301 7600; www.goldon27.com; 27th fl, Burj Al Arab, Umm Suqeim 3; ⏱6pm-2am; 📶; Ⓜ Mall of the Emirates)

Folly by Nick & Scott BAR

16 Ⓜ MAP P92, A1

This sprawling multistorey venue has a woodsy interior with an open kitchen, but it's really the three bars with killer views of the Burj Al Arab that steal the show (especially the tower). It's another venture by award-winning local chefs Nick Alvis and Scott Price, so expect quality nibbles to go with your cocktails, beer or biodynamic wines. (📞04 430 8535; www.folly.ae; Souk Madinat Jumeirah, King Salman Bin Abdulaziz Al Saud St, Umm Suqeim 3; ⏱noon-2.30pm & 5-11pm Sun-Thu, noon-3.30pm & 5-11pm Fri & Sat; 📶; Ⓜ Mall of the Emirates)

Entertainment

Cinema Akil CINEMA

17 ⭐ MAP P92, G5

Treating cine buffs to smart indie flicks from around the world on a pop-up basis since 2014, this dynamic platform has now taken up permanent residence at Alserkal Avenue. Screenings generally take place from 4pm on weekends and 7.30pm on weekdays and are often followed by Q&A sessions with directors. (www.cinema akil.com; 68 Alserkal Ave, Al Quoz 1; Ⓜ Al Safa, Umm Al Seef)

Madinat Theatre   THEATRE

18 ⭐ MAP P92, B1

The program at this handsome 442-seat theatre at Souk Madinat Jumeirah is largely calibrated to the cultural cravings of British expats. Expect plenty of crowd-pleasing entertainment ranging from popular West End imports to stand-up comedy, toe-tapping musicals and the annual panto. (🖉04 366 6546; www.madinattheatre.com; Souk Madinat Jumeirah, King Salman Bin Abdulaziz Al Saud St, Umm Suqeim 3; Ⓜ Mall of the Emirates)

Shopping

Mall of the Emirates   SHOPPING CENTRE

19 🔒 MAP P92, C5

Home to Ski Dubai (p95), a community theatre, a 24-screen multiplex cinema and – let's not forget – 630 shops, Mall of the Emirates is one of Dubai's most popular shopping centres. With narrow walkways, it can feel a tad claustrophobic at peak times (except in the striking Fashion Dome, lidded by a vaulted glass ceiling). (🖉04 409 9000; www.malloftheemirates.com; Sheikh Zayed Rd, Al Barsha; Ⓒ10am-10pm Sun-Wed, to midnight Thu-Sat; 🛜; Ⓜ Mall of the Emirates)

Camel Company   GIFTS & SOUVENIRS

20 🔒 MAP P92, B2

Hands-down the best spot for kid-friendly camel souvenirs: stuffed camels in all sizes and colours, camels on T-shirts, coffee cups, notebooks, greeting cards, fridge magnets – if you can slap a camel on it, Camel Company has done it. (🖉04 368 6048; www.camelcompany.ae; Souk Madinat Jumeirah, King Salman Bin Abdulaziz Al Saud St, Umm Suqeim 3; Ⓒ10am-11pm; 🛜; Ⓜ Mall of the Emirates)

O' de Rose   FASHION & ACCESSORIES

21 🔒 MAP P92, F4

Enjoy a sip of rose water upon entering this quirky concept boutique run by a trio of free-spirited cousins from Beirut. They share a passion for unusual things, as reflected in the store's eclectic line-up of ethnic-chic clothing, accessories, and art and home decor, most of it created by indie designers from around the region. (🖉04 348 7990; www.o-derose.com; 999 Al Wasl Rd, Umm Suqeim 2; Ⓒ10am-8pm Sat-Thu; Ⓜ Al Safa, Umm Al Seef)

Gold & Diamond Park   JEWELLERY

22 🔒 MAP P92, D5

An air-conditioned, less atmospheric alternative to the Deira Gold Souq, this buttoned-up business mall houses some 90 purveyors of bling. No bargaining here. If you can't find what you want, it's possible to commission a bespoke piece and have it ready in a couple of days. Refuel at the cafes ringing an outdoor courtyard. (🖉04 362 7777; www.goldanddiamondpark.com; Sheikh Zayed Rd; Ⓒ10am-10pm Sat-Thu, from 4pm Fri; Ⓜ Umm Al Seef)

Explore ◎

Downtown Dubai

Dubai's vibrant and urban centrepiece is anchored by the 828m-high Burj Khalifa, the world's tallest structure, and also brims with other distinctive and futuristic architecture, especially along Sheikh Zayed Rd where the Museum of the Future is the newest head-turning landmark.

Burj Khalifa overlooks the Dubai Mall, one of the world's biggest shopping temples with 1200 shops and such crowd-pleasing attractions as a three-storey aquarium, an ice rink and a dinosaur skeleton. The mall flanks the Burj Lake where the mesmerising Dubai Fountain erupts in choreographed dance, music and light shows nightly. For front-row views, book a table at a mall restaurant or head to the Time Out Market in the Arabian-themed Souk Al Bahar. There are also good views from the rooftop of the striking new Dubai Opera.

To tap into Dubai's creative scene, swing by the Dubai Design District or head straight to the hip Alserkal Avenue complex. Right in the gritty, industrial district of Al Quoz, the latter is a cluster of warehouses-turned-innovative art campus with cutting-edge galleries alongside hipster cafes, a community theatre, a chocolate factory, an art-house cinema and other creative enterprises. For more regional art, scan the prestigious galleries at Gate Village at the monumental Dubai International Financial Centre.

Getting There & Around

Dubai Metro's Red Line runs the entire length of Sheikh Zayed Rd. Major stations are Financial Centre, Emirates Towers, Burj Khalifa/Dubai Mall, Al Safa and Umm Al Seef.

Neighbourhood Map on p108

Burj Khalifa (p102) LUCIANO MORTULA/SHUTTERSTOCK © ARCHITECT: ADRIAN SMITH

Top Experience 📷
Enjoy the Views from Burj Khalifa

The Burj Khalifa is a ground-breaking feat of architecture and engineering with two observation decks on the 124th and 148th floors as well as the At.mosphere restaurant-bar on the 122nd. The world's tallest building pierces the sky at 828m (seven times the height of Big Ben); it opened in 2010, and only took six years to build. Up to 13,000 workers toiled day and night, putting up a new floor in as little as three days.

◎ MAP P108, D3

📞 800 2884 3867

www.atthetop.ae

lower ground fl, Dubai Mall, 1 Mohammed Bin Rashid Blvd

Ⓜ Burj Khalifa/Dubai Mall

Construction

Engineers and the Chicago-based architecture firm Skidmore, Owings & Merrill (SOM) had to pull out all the stops in the construction of the Burj Khalifa. Pouring the 11.5ft (3.5m) thick foundation alone required 16,350 cubic yards (12,500 cubic metres) of reinforced concrete. The design was inspired by the *Hymenocallis* desert lily. Refurbishments are planned, but specifics are being kept under wraps.

At the Top Observation Deck

Taking in the views from the world's tallest building is a deservedly crave-worthy experience and a trip to the **At the Top** observation deck (pictured) on the 124th floor (452m) is the most popular way to do it. Use high-powered 'viewfinders' that bring even distant developments into focus (at least on clear days) and cleverly simulate the same view at night and in the 1980s. In addition, digital telescopes with HD cameras zero in on places outside the cityscape. Getting to the deck means passing various multimedia exhibits until a double-decker lift zips you up at 10m per second.

At the Top Sky

To truly be on the world's highest observation platform, though, you need to buy tickets to **At the Top Sky** (555m). A visit here is set up like a hosted VIP experience with refreshments, a guided tour and an interactive screen where you 'fly' to different city landmarks by hovering your hands over high-tech sensors. Afterwards, you're escorted to the 125th floor to be showered with Burj trivia and take in another attraction called 'A Falcon's Eye View' that lets you take a virtual flight over the emirate by soaring over key attractions like a bird.

★ Top Tips

o Timed tickets are available at the ticket counter and often sell out quickly. Better to book online up to 30 days in advance.

o Book especially early if you want to go up at sunset.

o On hazy days, it's better to visit at night.

o Budget at least two hours for your visit.

o No refunds or rain checks are given if the outdoor viewing terrace is closed for bad weather.

o Prices go up during prime hours (around sunset) and closing times may vary depending on demand and the season.

✕ Take a Break

For fresh organic salads and mains with a view of the Burj and the lake, head to Baker & Spice (p112).

Top Experience 📷

Shop, Eat and Play at Dubai Mall

The 'mother of all malls' is much more than the sum of its 1200 stores: it's a village-sized family entertainment centre with a three-storey aquarium, a genuine dinosaur skeleton, indoor theme parks, state-of-the-art cinemas and an Olympic-sized ice rink. It also boasts a pretty souq and a designer fashion avenue with catwalk. More than 150 food outlets provide sustenance, some with outside terraces for front-row views of the Dubai Fountain and the Burj Khalifa.

◉ MAP P108, D3

☑ 800 382 246 255

www.thedubaimall.com

Sheikh Mohammed Bin Rashid Blvd

🕐 10am-midnight Mon-Thu, to 1am Fri-Sun

Ⓜ Burj Khalifa/Dubai Mall

Dubai Fountain

In a lake flanked by the Burj Khalifa and Dubai Mall, these spectacular dancing **fountains** (☎04 362 7500; www.thedubaimall.com/en/entertain-detail/the-dubai-fountain-1; Burj Lake; admission free; ⏰shows 1pm & 1.30pm Sat-Thu, 1.30pm & 2pm Fri, every 30min 6pm-midnight daily; Ⓜ Burj Khalifa/Dubai Mall) elicit oohs and aahs from young and old and are especially impressive after dark. Jets shooting up to 140m high are choreographed to move to a rotating roster of Western, Arabic and classical rhythms. The viewing area outside the Dubai Mall usually gets jam-packed. Tip: reserve a terrace table at one of the restaurants here or in Souk Al Bahar.

Dubai Aquarium & Underwater Zoo

About 75cm of plexiglass separates the rays, sharks, clownfish, groupers and around 250 other species of this **aquarium** (☎04 448 5200; www.thedubaiaquarium.com; ground fl, Dubai Mall, Sheikh Mohammed Bin Rashid Blvd; packages Dhs120-315; ⏰10am-11pm Sun-Wed, to midnight Thu-Sat; Ⓟ ⓘ; Ⓜ Burj Khalifa/Dubai Mall; pictured) from its visitors. Three storeys high and in the middle of the mall, the giant tank recreates an underwater habitat complete with artificial coral reefs and rocks. It's free to view from outside but you'll need tickets to access the walk-through tunnel and the upstairs Underwater Zoo where you can pay your respect to King Croc, a 5.1m-long crocodile, and his companion, Queen Croc.

Dubai Dino

Dubai's oldest denizen could hardly have imagined that he would make the trip from Wyoming to the Gulf some 155 million years after his death. Unearthed in 2008, the 24m-long and 7.6m-high dinosaur skeleton has held court among the sweeping arches of the Souk Dome since 2014.

★ Top Tips

○ Pick up a map and store directory from one of the staffed information desks or consult the interactive store finders.

○ Dubai Mall is busiest on Friday and Saturday evenings.

○ For close-ups of the Dubai Fountain show, board an abra (traditional boat) that sets sail for 25-minute rides between 5.45pm and 11.30pm (Dhs65).

✖ Take a Break

Ice-cream fans will be in ecstasy over the creamy flavours of **Morelli's Gelato** (☎04 339 9053; www.morellisgelato.com; lower ground fl, scoop Dhs20; ⏰10am-midnight; Ⓟ 🛜).

Top Experience 📷

Marvel at the Museum of the Future

Open since 22.02.2022, this eye-opening museum fast-forwards visitors 50 years into the future and aims to spark discussions about the scientific and technological advancements humans might achieve by 2071. It's housed in an architecturally stunning building adorned with poetic Arabic calligraphy. The void within its elliptical shape is meant to evoke a human eye looking toward the future.

◉ MAP P108, G2

www.museumofthe future.ae

Sheikh Zayed Rd & Trade Center St

adult/child under 3 Dhs145/free

🕙 10am-6pm

Ⓜ Emirates Towers

Exhibits

Exploring the seven floors of interactive exhibits taps into all five senses to imagine what vast possibilities the future might hold. Venture to a space station 600 miles above the earth to imagine how the moon could be transformed to provide renewable energy for the earth. Another spot whisks you to a digital Amazon rainforest where you can observe different species, including some that are not usually visible to the human eye. Other floors shine the spotlight on the future of transportation, health, food and water, while the top floor hosts a dedicated section for children called 'Future Heroes'. Modelled after video games, the exhibit allows children to become players, problem-solving to conquer challenges and collecting badges for their achievements.

Should you experience digital overwhelm, there's even a 'sanctuary' to help you 'disconnect from technology and reconnect with mind, body and spirit'.

Architecture

Perched atop a grassy mound, the museum itself is an engineering marvel and an eyecatcher along Sheikh Zayed Rd. Each part of its design is a nod to the scientific innovation it wishes to inspire. The building's skin consists of 1,024 stainless steel panels, which happens to be the number of bytes in a kilobyte, the basic unit of digital storage in a computer. Each of these panels was uniquely crafted using algorithms and robots to 3D map more than 14,000 metres of Arabic script. The calligraphy consists of three poems penned by Dubai's ruler Sheikh Mohammed himself.

★ Top Tips

○ You must have a ticket for a timed entry into the museum.

○ Book your tickets two weeks in advance at https://museumofthefuture.ae/en/book

✖ Take a Break

Head to Noodle House (p117) for its pan-Asian menu, or Zaroob (p113) for a taste of Lebanon street food.

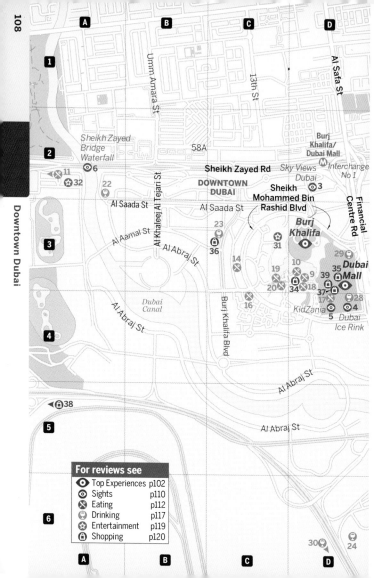

Downtown Dubai

A   B   C   D

1

1

Sheikh Zayed Bridge Waterfall

◎6

◀☆11
☆32

22
❓

Umm Amara St

13th St

Al Safa St

58A

Burj Khalifa/ Dubai Mall

Ⓜ Interchange No 1

Sky Views Dubai
◎3

Sheikh Zayed Rd

DOWNTOWN DUBAI

Al Khaleej Al Tejari St

Al Saada St

Al Saada St

Sheikh Mohammed Bin Rashid Blvd

Financial Centre Rd

Al Aamal St

23
🔒
36

Burj Khalifa
◉

Al Abraj St

☆31

14
✖

19
✖
20✖

10

34
🔒

9
🔒

39
🔒

18
🔒

29🔒

35
🔒

Dubai Mall
◉

37🔒

17🔒

28
🔒

Dubai Canal

Burj Khalifa Blvd

16
✖

5
◉

KidZania

4
◉

Dubai Ice Rink

Al Abraj St

Al Abraj St

Al Abraj St

◀🔒38

5

6

30▶🔒

24
🍴

For reviews see	
◉ Top Experiences	p102
◎ Sights	p110
✖ Eating	p112
🍴 Drinking	p117
☆ Entertainment	p119
🔒 Shopping	p120

A   B   C   D

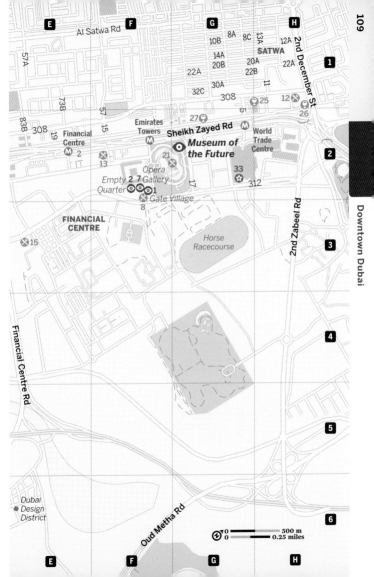

E · Al Satwa Rd · F

G

H · 2nd December St

57A

10B · 8A · 8C · 13A · 12A

1

SATWA

14A · 20A · 22A

22A · 20B · 22B

73B · 30A · 11

32C · 308 · 5

57 · 15 · ✕13 25 · ✕12 26

83B · 308 · 19 · Financial Centre · M 2

Emirates Towers · ✕27 · Sheikh Zayed Rd · M · Museum of the Future · World Trade Centre

2

M · 21 · 33 · 312

Opera Gallery · ✕17

Empty Quarter · 2 7

1 · Gate Village

8

FINANCIAL CENTRE

✕15

Horse Racecourse

3

2nd Zabeel Rd

4

Financial Centre Rd

5

Dubai Design District

Oud Metha Rd

6

0 — 500 m
0 — 0.25 miles

Sights

Gate Village
AREA

1 MAP P108, F2

Two wooden bridges link the massive Dubai International Finance Centre to Gate Village, a modernist cluster of 10 midrise stone-clad towers built around walkways and small piazzas. This is where many of Dubai's high-end Middle Eastern art galleries, including **Ayyam** (☎ 04 323 6242; www.ayyamgallery.com; Unit B11, Alserkal Ave, Al Quoz 1; ⏰ 10am-6pm Sun-Thu, from noon Sat; Ⓜ Al Safa, Umm Al Seef), have set up shop alongside upmarket restaurants like Zuma (p112) and Cipriani. Note that the place is all but dead on weekends. (Happiness St; Ⓟ; Ⓜ Emirates Towers)

Empty Quarter
GALLERY

2 MAP P108, F2

It's always worth stopping by this top-notch gallery, which is the only one in the UAE focused entirely on fine-art photography. While providing a platform for emerging talent, curators also put on shows featuring top international shutterbugs like Steve McCurry, Bruno Barbey, Marc Riboud and Al Moutasim Al Maskery. Many capture the zeitgeist with evocative, provocative or political themes.

It's part of the Gate Village gallery district at DIFC. (☎ 04 323 1210; www.theemptyquarter.com; Bldg 2, Gate Village, DIFC; ⏰ 10am-7pm Sun-Thu; Ⓟ; Ⓜ Emirates Towers)

Sky Views Dubai
ADVENTURE SPORTS

3 MAP P108, D2

Not recommended for the vertigo-prone, this elevated experience has you walking 220 metres in the air via a glass bridge linking the two towers of The Address Sky View hotel, followed by zipping down one floor in an exterior transparent tube. True dare-devils can strap into a harness and take an 'Edge Walk' – a saunter along a

Dubai Design District

The fresh-off-the-drawing board **Dubai Design District** (d3; Map p108, E6; ☎ 04 433 3000; www.dubaidesigndistrict.com; off Al Khail Rd, Business Bay; Ⓟ; 🚌 Dubai Design District, Ⓜ Business Bay) has attracted both regional and international talent and brands, including hot shots like Adidas and Foster + Partners. Visitors can tap into this laboratory of tastemakers by checking out the edgy architecture and public art, browsing showrooms and pop-ups, eavesdropping on bearded hipsters in sleek cafes, or attending a free cultural event. It's 20 minutes by bus D03 or D03A from Dubai Mall/Burj Khalifa metro station.

PHILIP LANGE/SHUTTERSTOCK ©

Sheikh Zayed Bridge Waterfall (p112)

lofty alfresco ledge encircling the hotel. (📞 04 873 8888; www.sky viewsdubai.com; Emaar Sq Area; adult/child Dhs85/60, Edge Walk Dhs714; 🕙10am-10pm; Ⓜ Burj Khalifa/Dubai Mall)

Dubai Ice Rink   ICE SKATING

4 ◉ MAP P108, D4

This Olympic-sized ice rink inside Dubai Mall is ringed with cafes and restaurants and can even be converted into a concert arena. Sign up for a private or group class if you're a little wobbly in the knees. There is a separate area to enjoy the half-hour Icebyke experience, basically a skating/cycling combo that promises to glide you seamlessly across the ice. There are DJ sessions for families in the afternoons; other cool activities include

night-time discos. (📞 04 437 1111; www.dubaiicerink.com; ground fl, Dubai Mall; per session incl skates Dhs75-100, Icebyke Dhs80; 🕙10am-midnight; 🛝; Ⓜ Burj Khalifa/Dubai Mall)

KidZania   AMUSEMENT PARK

5 ◉ MAP P108, D4

For guilt-free shopping without your kids, drop them off in this indoor miniature city – complete with a school, a fire station, a hospital and a bank – where they get to dress up and slip into adult roles to playfully explore what it's like to be a firefighter, a doctor, a mechanic, a pilot or other professional. (📞 04 448 5222; www.kidzania.ae; 2nd fl, Dubai Mall; tickets from Dhs180; 🕙10am-11pm; Ⓟ🛝; Ⓜ Burj Khalifa/Dubai Mall)

Sheikh Zayed Bridge Waterfall   WATERFALL

6 ◉ MAP P108, A2

This illuminated and motion-operated waterfall cascades down both sides of Sheikh Zayed Bridge, stopping only for passing vessels. It's an impressive sight to enjoy while strolling alongside the canal. (Dubai Canal, Sheikh Zayed Bridge; admission free; ☺7-10pm; Ⓜ Business Bay)

Opera Gallery   GALLERY

7 ◉ MAP P108, F2

More an art showroom than a classically curated gallery, Opera caters to collectors of artistic heavyweights in genres as varied as pop art, calligraphy and landscapes. One section of the striking bilevel space is reserved for contemporary artists from the Middle East.

Opera was founded in Paris in 1994; the Dubai branch is one of a dozen around the world. (☎04 323 0909; www.operagallery.com; Bldg 3, Gate Village; ☺10am-10pm Sun-Wed, to midnight Thu, 2-9pm Fri, 11am-9pm Sat; Ⓜ Emirates Towers)

Eating

Zuma   JAPANESE $$$

8 ✗ MAP P108, F2

Every dish speaks of refinement in this perennially popular bi-level restaurant that gives classic Japanese fare an up-to-the-minute workout. No matter if you go for the top-cut sushi morsels (the dynamite spider roll is a serious eye-catcher!), meat and seafood on the robata grill, or such signature dishes as miso-marinated black cod, you'll be keeping your taste buds happy. (☎04 425 5660; www.zumarestaurant.com; Bldg 06, Gate Village, Happiness St, DIFC; set lunches Dhs130, mains Dhs115-850; ☺noon-3.30pm Mon-Fri, 12.30-4pm Sat & Sun, plus 7pm-midnight Sun-Wed, to 1am Thu-Sat; 🛜; Ⓜ Emirates Towers)

Baker & Spice   INTERNATIONAL $$

9 ✗ MAP P108, D3

A pioneer of the local-organic-fresh maxim in Dubai, this London import offers a seasonal bounty of dishes, prepared in-house and served amid charming, country-style decor and on a Dubai Fountain–facing terrace. The salad bar brims with inspired creations, the breakfasts are tops, and the meat and fish dishes sustainably sourced. (☎04 425 2240; www.bakerandspiceme.com; Souk Al Bahar; mains Dhs80-100; ☺8am-11pm; 🛜✎; Ⓜ Burj Khalifa/Dubai Mall)

Time Out Market   FOOD HALL $$

10 ✗ MAP P108, D3

Silky ramen to smoky brisket, tangy ceviche to crispy falafel – at this high-octane food hall, you can send your tastebuds around the globe without a passport. The vast, brick-pillared space at Souk Al Bahar harnesses the tastes and talents of 18 locally adored culinary outposts (plus three bars).

Dining in Thin Air: At.mosphere

The food may not be out of this world, but the views are certainly stellar from the world's highest restaurant (442m) in the **Burj Khalifa** (p102). Book far ahead to enjoy the views and international fare with an emphasis on seafood. The per-person minimum spend in the restaurant is Dhs500 at lunch and Dhs680 for dinner (Dhs880 for window table). If that's too dear, head one floor up to the lounge level where minimums are Dhs200 for breakfast, Dhs420 for afternoon tea and Dhs320 for dinner. No children under 10 are allowed. Dress nicely. The entrance is through the Armani Hotel.

Best seat: on the terrace next to Dubai Fountain. (www.timeout market.com/dubai; 3rd fl, Souk Al Bahar, Old Town Island; mains from Dhs50; ⏰noon-midnight Mon-Thu, noon-1am Fri, 10am-1am Sat, 10am-midnight Sun; P❄️🚻; MBurj Khalifa/Dubai Mall)

Nightjar Coffee
CAFE $

11 🗺 MAP P108, A2

New Zealander Leon Surynt works directly with cocoa bean farmers, ensuring sustainability and fairness. There is a similar vision behind the menu, with ingredients locally sourced as far as possible. Dishes are based on local staples with a dash of innovation, such as ox tongue with comte and onion jam, spiced lamb shoulder, and grilled cauliflower with Darjeeling pickled raisins and pine nuts.

Stepping into the dining room here is a little like stepping into a giant cocoa bean, with dark wood furnishings and low lighting. (📞50 518 1768; www.nightjar.coffee; Alserkal Ave, Al Quoz 1; dishes Dhs25-50;

⏰9am-9pm Mon-Sat, to 6pm Sun; 📶; MAl Safa, Umm Al Seef)

Sum of Us
CAFE $$

12 🗺 MAP P108, H1

This two-floor industrial-style and plant-filled cafe with outdoor seating roasts its own beans, bakes its own sourdough bread and serves food that is at once comforting and exciting. All-day breakfast choices include French toast with salted caramel sauce, while the cauliflower risotto makes for an interesting main dish. (📞056 445 7526; www.thesumofusdubai.com; ground fl, Burj Al Salam Bldg, 6th St; mains Dhs50-90; ⏰8am-11pm; P📶🚲; MWorld Trade Centre)

Zaroob
LEBANESE $

13 🗺 MAP P108, F2

With its live cooking stations, open kitchens, fruit-filled baskets, colourful lanterns and graffiti-covered steel shutters, Zaroob radiates the urban integrity of a Beirut street-food alley. Feast on such delicious no-fuss food as falafel, shawarma (spit-roasted meat in pita bread), flat or wrapped *manoushe* (Levant-style pizza) or *alayet* (tomato stew), all typical of the Levant. Nice terrace too. (📞04 327 6262; www.zaroob.com; Shop 1, Jumeirah Tower Bldg, Sheikh Zayed Rd; dishes Dhs12-32; ⏱24hr; 🅿 🛜 🍴; Ⓜ Emirates Towers, Financial Centre)

Leila
LEBANESE $$

14 ✖ MAP P108, C3

This Beirut import serves granny-style rural Lebanese cafe cuisine adapted for the 21st century: light, healthy and fresh. The homey decor more than dabbles in the vintage department with its patterned wallpaper, crisp tablecloths and floral crockery. It's also a nice spot for breakfast and shisha. (📞04 448 3384; www.leilarestaurant.ae; Sheikh Mohammed Bin Rashid Blvd; mains Dhs50-68; ⏱9.30am-12.45am Mon-Fri, to 1.45am Sat & Sun; 🛜; Ⓜ Burj Khalifa/Dubai Mall)

The Daily
BISTRO $$

15 ✖ MAP P108, E3

Warehouse-style decor, floor-to-ceiling windows and an outdoor terrace – overlooking Burj Khalifa, no less – make an instant impression at this casual all-day spot. Add in warm service and easy-going food (shakshuka eggs, superfood salads, steak and chips) at very reasonable prices, and you know you're onto a winner. Wash it down with fresh juices, barista-made coffee and well-priced beer

and wine. (📞04 561 9999; www.rovehotels.com/the-daily; Rove Downtown, 312 Happiness St; mains Dhs45-120, brunch Dhs99; ⏱6.30am-11.30pm; 🛜; Ⓜ Financial Centre, Burj Khalifa/Dubai Mall)

La Serre Bistro & Boulangerie
MEDITERRANEAN $$$

16 ✖ MAP P108, C4

Downtown residents regularly swing by the downstairs *boulangerie* (bakery) for buttery croissants, toothsome pastries or *petit déjeuner* (breakfast) on the terrace at this Parisian-inspired cafe, while gourmets on a spending spree head one floor up to tuck into black truffle pasta, caviar and turbot and other fanciful dishes in the breezy bistro dining room. (📞04 428 6969; www.laserre.com; Vida Downtown Dubai, Sheikh Mohammed Bin Rashid Blvd; bistro mains Dhs135-325; ⏱bistro noon-3.30pm & 7-11.30pm, boulangerie 6.30am-10pm; 🅿 🛜 🍴; Ⓜ Burj Khalifa/Dubai Mall)

Eataly
ITALIAN $$

17 ✖ MAP P108, D4

Italy's popular shop-cafe has landed in Dubai Mall, bringing artisanal morsels from around the Boot to discerning palates. Stock up on pesto from Liguria, balsamico from Modena, olive oil from Sicily, and mozzarella and pasta made right in the store. Alternatively, stay and enjoy delicious pizza, panini or pasta freshly prepared at several food stations.

For kids, it's fun to watch the action and perhaps finish up the meal with a trip to the Nutella bar. (📞04 330 8899; www.eatalyarabia. com; lower ground fl, Dubai Mall; mains Dhs45-120; ⏰9am-11.30pm Sun-Wed, to 12.30am Thu-Sat; 🅿 📶 ♿; Ⓜ Burj Khalifa/Dubai Mall)

Karma Kafé ASIAN $$$

18 🍴 MAP P108, D3

Look for the large Buddha guarding the dining room dressed in sensuous burgundy with gold leaf accents. The menu hopscotches around Asia with classic and innovative sushi alongside such mains as tea-smoked salmon, Wagyu beef sliders from the robata grill, and black miso cod. The terrace has sublime Dubai Fountain views.

Vegetarians may feel slightly faint at the veg-marked dish: *caterpillar signature rolls*. No worries, these are actually filled with shitake mushrooms, asparagus, avocado and other vegetables. Phew! (📞04 423 0909; www. karma-kafe.com; Souk Al Bahar; mains Dhs85-270; ⏰3pm-2am Sun-Thu, from noon Fri & Sat; 📶; Ⓜ Burj Khalifa/Dubai Mall)

Asado ARGENTINE $$$

19 🍴 MAP P108, C3

Meat lovers will be in heaven at this rustic-elegant lair with stellar views of the Burj Khalifa from the terrace tables. Start with a selection of stuffed empanadas before treating yourself to a juicy grilled Argentine steak or the signature baby goat, slowly tickled

Baker & Spice (p112)

Downtown Dubai Eating

Religion on a Plate

A Question of Pork

Muslims don't eat pork: it is *haram*, forbidden by Islam, as pigs are considered unclean. Alcohol is forbidden because it makes followers forgetful of God and prayer. The other major dietary restriction applies to meat: it must be halal, meaning religiously suitable or permitted. The animal must be drained of its blood at the time of slaughter by having its throat cut. That is why much of the red meat slaughtered and sold locally is very pale in colour. In restaurants, you will easily find nonhalal beef – just don't expect your tenderloin to be wrapped in a fatty strip of bacon before it's grilled.

Restaurants & Supermarkets

Some supermarkets sell beef and turkey bacon as an alternative to pork bacon, though hypermarkets such as Carrefour and Spinneys have dedicated 'pork rooms' that sell the real thing – they may not officially be entered by Muslims. To serve pork in a restaurant, you must have a pork licence. Likewise with alcohol, which is generally only served in hotels. If an item on a restaurant menu has been prepared with either alcohol or pork, it must be clearly marked.

Ramadan

The holy month of Ramadan is a time of spiritual contemplation for Muslims, who must fast from sunrise to sunset. Non-Muslim visitors are not expected to fast, but they should not smoke, drink or eat (including gum-chewing) in public during daylight hours. Business premises and hotels make provisions for the nonfasting by erecting screens around dining areas.

Ramadan would seem to be the ideal time to lose weight, yet lots of people pile on the pounds. The fast is broken each day with a communal breakfast comprising something light (such as dates and laban – an unsweetened yoghurt drink) before prayers. Then comes *iftar* at which enough food is usually consumed to compensate for the previous hours of abstinence with socialising that continues well into the early hours. With hundreds of restaurants putting on good-value *iftar* buffets, the temptation to overindulge is everywhere.

to succulent perfection on an outdoor charcoal grill. Reservations essential. (📞04 428 7888; www. addresshotels.com/en/restaurant/ asado; ground fl, Palace Downtown, Mohammed Bin Rashid Blvd; mains Dhs95-570; ⏰6.30-11.30pm; 🅿🛜; Ⓜ Burj Khalifa/Dubai Mall)

Thiptara at Palace Downtown

THAI $$$

20 MAP P108, C3

Thiptara means 'magic at the water' – very appropriate given its romantic setting in a lakeside pagoda with unimpeded views of the Dubai Fountain. The menu presents elegant interpretations of classic Thai dishes perked up by herbs grown by the chef himself.

The green papaya salad, grilled black cod and green chicken curry are all solid menu picks. (04 428 7888; www.addresshotels.com/en/restaurant/Thiptara; Mohammed Bin Rashid Blvd; mains Dhs120-290; 6-11.30pm; P; M Burj Khalifa/Dubai Mall)

Noodle House

ASIAN $$

21 MAP P108, G2

This multibranch pan-Asian restaurant is a reliably good choice for a casual lunch or dinner. There's great variety – from roast duck to noodle soups, nasi goreng and pad Thai – and a spice-level indicator to please disparate tastes.

Other branches include Souk Madinat Jumeirah, Dubai Mall and DIFC. See the website for details. (04 319 8088; www.thenoodlehouse.com; ground fl, Boulevard Mall, Emirates Towers, Sheikh Zayed Rd; mains Dhs35-90; noon-midnight; P; M Emirates Towers)

Drinking

Bridgewater Tavern

SPORTS BAR

22 MAP P108, A2

This happening joint has ushered the sports bar into a new era. Sure, there are the requisite big screens to catch the action, but it's packaged into an industrial-flavoured space with (mostly) rock on the turntables, shisha on the canalside terrace, and an elevated gastropub menu whose signature 'black' burger is so messy it comes with a bib. (04 414 0000; www.jwmarriottmarquisdubailife.com/dining/bridgewatertavern; JW Marriott Marquis Hotel, Sheikh Zayed Rd; 4pm-2am; ; M Business Bay)

Treehouse

BAR

23 MAP P108, C3

At the top of the Taj, this luxe lair treats guests to cracking views of the Burj Khalifa, top-shelf drinks and an outdoor living room setting with potted plants, pillow-packed sofas, pink marble tables and even a candlelit mock fireplace. A chill spot for quiet conversation on weekdays, the action picks up with deep-house DJs on weekends.

On a culinary note, the Treehouse is also gaining steam for its barbecue and sushi **Secret Wonderland Brunch** extravaganza on Saturdays (from Dhs299). (04 438 3100; www.treehousedubai.ae; Taj Dubai Hotel, Burj Khalifa Blvd; 6pm-2am Sun-Thu, to 3am Fri & Sat; ; M Business Bay)

Base
CLUB

24 ⬤ MAP P108, D6

This b-i-g next-gen nightclub holds forth under open skies in the Dubai Design District and can host up to 5000 people for concerts and parties. Expect a top-notch sound system, a top line-up, pyrotechnics, platforms for dancers and shiny happy people. (☏055 313 4999; www.basedubai.com; Dubai Design District; ⏱10.30am-3am Sep-May; Ⓜ Business Bay)

Cavalli Club
CLUB

25 ⬤ MAP P108, H1

Black limos jostle for position outside this over-the-top lair where you can sip Italian fashion designer Roberto Cavalli's vodka-based cocktails and dine on Italian fare served on Cavalli plates with Cavalli cutlery amid a virtual Aladdin's cave of black quartz and Swarovski crystals. Ladies, wear those vertiginous heels or risk feeling frumpy. Men, dress snappily or forget about it.

The entrance is behind the hotel. (☏050 991 0400; http://dubai.cavalliclub.com; Fairmont Hotel, Sheikh Zayed Rd; ⏱8.30pm-3am; 🛜; Ⓜ World Trade Centre)

40 Kong
BAR

26 ⬤ MAP P108, H1

Finance moguls and corporate execs mix it up at this intimate rooftop cocktail bar perched atop the 40th floor of the H Hotel with views of the World Trade Centre and Sheikh Zayed Rd. The twinkling lanterns and palm trees set romantic accents for post-work or post-shopping sundowners, paired with global bar bites. (☏04 355 8896; www.40kong.com; 40th fl, H Hotel, Sheikh Zayed Rd; ⏱7pm-3am; 🛜; Ⓜ World Trade Centre)

Fibber Magee's
IRISH PUB

27 ⬤ MAP P108, G2

Been-around-forever Fibbers is an amiably scruffy morning-to-night Irish pub with Guinness and Kilkenny on tap, all-day breakfasts (including the legendary breakfast bap), plus a menu of international comfort food designed to keep brains in balance, and sports (rugby to horse racing) on the big screens. Traditional Irish music on Thursday nights puts a tear in many expat eyes. (☏04 332 2400; www.fibbersdubai.com; Saeed Tower One, Sheikh Zayed Rd; ⏱8am-2am; 🛜; Ⓜ World Trade Centre)

Majlis
CAFE

28 ⬤ MAP P108, D4

If you ever wanted to find out how to milk a camel (and who doesn't?), watch the video on the interactive iPad menu of this pretty cafe while sipping a camelccino (camel-milk cappuccino) or date-flavoured camel milk. Nibbles, desserts, chocolate and cheese, all made with camel milk, beckon as well. (☏056 287 1522; ground fl, The Souk, Dubai Mall; ⏱10am-midnight; 🛜; Ⓜ Burj Khalifa/Dubai Mall)

Cabana

LOUNGE

29 MAP P108, D3

A laid-back poolside vibe combines with urban sophistication and stellar views of the Burj Khalifa at this al fresco restaurant and terrace lounge. A DJ plays smooth tunes that don't hamper animated conversation. Cap off a Dubai Mall shopping spree at happy hour, which runs from 2pm to 8pm. (📞04 438 8888; www.addresshotels.com/en/restaurant/cabana-2; 3rd fl, Address Dubai Mall Hotel, Sheikh Mohammed Bin Rashid Blvd; ⏲midday-4am; 🛜; Ⓜ Burj Khalifa/Dubai Mall)

White Dubai

CLUB

30 🚇 MAP P108, D6

The Dubai spawn of the Beirut original did not need long to lure local socialites with high-energy rooftop parties under the stars. International spinmeisters shower partygoers with an eclectic sound soup, from house and electro to bump-and-grind hip-hop and R&B, all fuelled by dazzling projections and light shows.

It's the only Middle Eastern club on the Top 100 list of the British *DJ Mag*. (📞050 443 0933; www.whitedubai.com; Meydan Racecourse Grandstand Rooftop, Nad Al Sheba; ⏲11pm-3am Tue, Thu-Sat; 🛜)

Entertainment

Dubai Opera

PERFORMING ARTS

31 ⭐ MAP P108, C3

Shaped like a traditional dhow – the sailing vessels that still ply the Gulf – Dubai Opera is the city's

Dubai Opera

LABORANT7/SHUTTERSTOCK © ARCHITECT: JANUS ROSTOCK

newest high-calibre performing-arts venue. Despite its name, it actually hosts a potpourri of shows, including musicals, ballet, comedy acts, rock bands and recitals. The 'bow' of the building contains a 2000-seat theatre and glass-fronted foyer overlooking Burj Lake. (📞04 440 8888; www.dubaiopera.com; Sheikh Mohammed Bin Rashid Blvd; Ⓜ Burj Khalifa/Dubai Mall)

La Perle by Dragone
PERFORMING ARTS

32 ⭐ MAP P108, A2

A custom-designed theatre with a 270-degree angle makes for perfect sight lines even in the cheaper seats of this magical show centred on an aquatic stage where some 65 acrobats perform their stunning stunts. It is the brainchild of Franco Dragone, one of the original creators of Cirque du Soleil. (www.laperle.com; Al Habtoor City; tickets Dhs400-1600; 📶; Ⓜ Business Bay)

Blue Bar
LIVE MUSIC

33 ⭐ MAP P108, G2

Cool cats of all ages gather in this relaxed joint for some of the finest live jazz and blues in town, along with a full, reasonably priced bar line-up that includes signature cocktails named after jazz greats (try the Louis Armstrong–inspired Hello Dolly) ordered on an iPad's interactive menu. It's open daily with live concerts from 10pm Thursday to Saturday. (📞04 310 8150; Novotel World Trade Centre Dubai, Happiness St; 🕐noon-2am; 📶; Ⓜ World Trade Centre)

Shopping

Souk Al Bahar
MALL

34 🔒 MAP P108, D3

Translated as 'market of the sailor', Souk Al Bahar is a small arabesque-style mall next to the Dubai Mall that sells mostly tourist-geared items. It's really more noteworthy for its enchanting design (arch-lined stone corridors, dim lighting) and Dubai Fountain–facing restaurants, some of which are licensed. Also handy: a branch of Spinneys supermarket in the basement. (www.soukalbahar.ae; Old Town Island; 🕐10am-10pm

Nayomi

Sun-Thu, from 2pm Fri; 🛜; Ⓜ Burj Khalifa/Dubai Mall)

Kinokuniya   BOOKS

35 🔒 MAP P108, D3

This massive shop is El Dorado for bookworms. Shelves are stocked with a mind-boggling half-a-million tomes plus 1000 or so magazines in English, Arabic, Japanese, French, German and Chinese. (📞 04 434 0111; www.kinokuniya.com/ae; 2nd fl, Dubai Mall; ⏱10am-midnight; 🛜; Ⓜ Burj Khalifa/Dubai Mall)

Farmers Market on the Terrace   MARKET

36 🔒 MAP P108, C3

The carrots may have roots attached and dirt might stick to the fennel bulb, because both were still in the ground the previous day. Now they're vying for customers at this small farmers market, which brings organic, locally grown produce straight from grower to grazer. (📞 04 427 9856; www.facebook.com/TheFarmers MarketOnTheTerrace; Bay Avenue Park, Burj Khalifa & Al A'amal Sts, Business Bay; ⏱8am-1pm Fri Nov-May; Ⓜ Business Bay)

Candylicious   FOOD

37 🔒 MAP P108, D3

Stand under the lollipop tree, watch the candy-makers at work or gorge yourself on gourmet popcorn at this colourful candy emporium stocked to the rafters with everything from jelly beans to halal sweets and gourmet chocolate. Sweet bliss. Just don't tell your dentist. (📞 04 330 8700; www.candyliciousshop.com; ground fl, Dubai Mall; ⏱10am-midnight; 🛜; Ⓜ Burj Khalifa/Dubai Mall)

Dubai Hills Mall   MALL

38 🔒 MAP P108, A5

Feeding shopping cravings at 600 stores is just one reason to swing by this mall in the upscale residential Dubai Hills neighbourhood. Another is an indoor coaster called 'The Storm' that kicks off with a spine-tingling vertical launch. Kiddies, meanwhile, can channel their inner Ninja or Spiderman in the 11 play areas of the Adventure Park. (📞 04 448 5033; www.dubaihillsmall.ae; Umm Suqeim & Al Khail Sts; ⏱10am-midnight daily; 🛜👫)

Nayomi   CLOTHING

39 🔒 MAP P108, D3

One of Dubai's raciest stores stocks push-up bras, high-heeled feathery slippers, slinky night gowns, seductive beauty products (we like the 'Booty Parlor' line) and other nocturnal niceties from – surprise! – Saudi Arabia. In fact, Nayomi, which means 'soft' and 'delicate' in Arabic, is a major brand all over the Middle East, with 10 branches around Dubai alone. (📞 04 339 8820; www.nayomi.com; 1st fl, Dubai Mall; ⏱10am-10pm Sun-Wed, to midnight Thu-Sat; 🛜; Ⓜ Burj Khalifa/Dubai Mall)

Explore

Dubai Marina & Palm Jumeirah

Dubai Marina has become one of the most popular places to live and visit. Carved from the desert, this is one of the world's largest marinas, centred on a 3km-long canal flanked by a thicket of futuristic high-rises, including the twisting Cayan Tower. A stroll along the Marina Walk promenade is delightful, especially after dusk when you can gaze out at the glittering towers and bobbing yachts and find your favourite dinner, drinks or shisha spot.

Paralleling the beach are The Walk at JBR, a 1.7km-long strip of shops and family-friendly eateries, and The Beach at JBR, a chic open-air mall fronting a lovely sandy beach with great infrastructure. Just offshore are Bluewaters Islands with the Ain Dubai observation wheel and the emerging Dubai Harbour neighbourhood. The Dubai Tram threads through much of the Marina.

Jutting into the Gulf is the Palm Jumeirah, an artificial island in the shape of a palm tree. Built to increase Dubai's beachfront, it's home to luxury apartments, villas and hotels and punctuated by the Atlantis The Palm resort with its aquarium and giant water park.

Further south lie the family-friendly theme parks of Dubai Parks & Resorts and the Expo 2020 grounds.

Getting There & Around

Dubai Metro's Red Line stops at Sobha Realty for the Dubai Marina. For The Walk at JBR, the DMCC station is a bit more convenient. Dubai Tram links Dubai Media City, JBR and Dubai Marina on an 11km loop. Palm Jumeirah is served by monorail.

Neighbourhood Map on p126

Palm Jumeirah MIKADA/GETTY IMAGES ©

Walking Tour

Dubai Marina Walk

Built around a 3km-long canal flanked by a thicket of futuristic high-rises, the Dubai Marina is one of the world's largest marinas. A saunter along its promenade is delightful, especially at night, when you can contemplate the shining towers and yachts, stop by the dancing fountains and stake out your favourite dinner and drink spot.

Walk Facts

Start Cayan Tower

End Barracuda

Length 2.5km; as long as you like

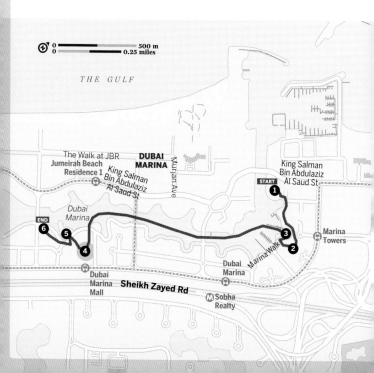

❶ Cayan Tower

This architectural **stunner** (Al Sharta St, Dubai Marina; M Sobha Realty, 🚊 Marina Towers) is quite literally a building with a twist as its 75 stories spiral over 307m at a 90-degree angle. Designed by Skidmore, Owings & Merrill (SOM), which also masterminded the Burj Khalifa, it is the most eye-catching in the phalanx of high-rises in the Dubai Marina.

❷ Bicycle Cruising

Nextbike (Byky; 📞 04 238 4344; www.nextbike.net; 1/2/5/24hr Dhs20/25/40/80; ⏰ 24hr) lets you pick up and drop off bicycles at numerous stations dotted around the Dubai Marina and Palm Jumeirah, including one next to Spinneys supermarket. All you need to do is register first via its website, which also has full details about how the scheme works.

❸ Water Bus

For a scenic spin around the marina, hop on the **Water Bus** (www. rta.ae; Dubai Marina; tickets Dhs3-11, 1-day pass Dhs25; ⏰ 10am-11pm Sat-Thu, noon-midnight Fri; M Sobha Realty, 🚊 Dubai Marina Mall), which shuttles between the Marina Walk, Marina Terrace, Marina Mall and the Promenade every 15 minutes. It's lovely at sunset or after dark when you float past the show-stopping parade of shimmering towers.

❹ Dubai Marina Mall

With only 140 stores, **Dubai Marina Mall** (p139) may not rank among the city's megamalls, yet the shops are just as good and you won't get lost quite so readily. Its main architectural feature is the giant atrium where kids can trundle around in a toy train.

❺ Gourmet Tower

The circular, seven-storey **Pier 7** (p132) is a feast for foodies, with each floor holding a hip restaurant or bar with terraces delivering stunning views of bobbing yachts and twinkling towers. Options include sizzling Asian at Asia Asia and rooftop cocktails at Atelier M.

❻ Seafood Feast

Empty tables are rare at **Barracuda** (📞 04 452 2278; www. barracuda-restaurant.com; Silverene Tower, Marina Walk, Dubai Marina; mains Dhs50-215; ⏰ noon-1am; 📶; M DMCC, 🚊 Dubai Marina Mall), an Egyptian seafood shrine where the catch of the day is theatrically displayed on ice. Options for having it prepared include an oven-grilled version simply drizzled with olive oil and lemon.

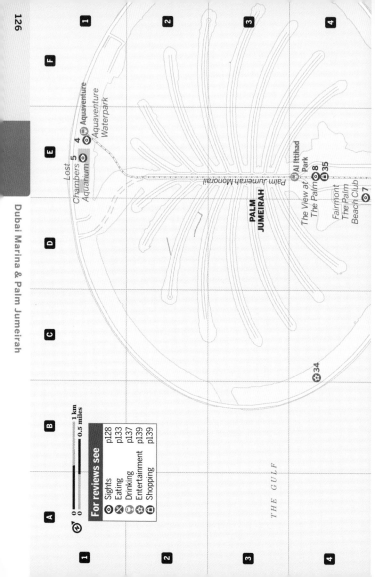

For reviews see

⊘ Sights	p128
✕ Eating	p133
🍷 Drinking	p137
🎭 Entertainment	p139
🛍 Shopping	p139

0 ─── 1 km
0 ─── 0.5 miles

Aquaventure
Waterpark

Aquaventure ⊙ **4**

Lost **5** ⊙
Chambers
Aquarium

Palm Jumeirah Monorail

**PALM
JUMEIRAH**

Al Ittihad
Park

The View at
The Palm ⊙ **8** 🛍 **35**

Fairmont
The Palm
Beach Club
🍷 **7**

☆ **34**

THE GULF

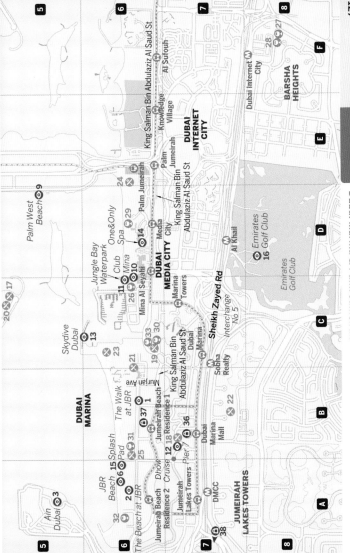

Dubai Marina & Palm Jumeirah

Ain Dubai ⊙3

The Beach at JBR

Jumeirah Beach Residence 2

JBR Beach

32

2⊙ 6⊙

15 Splash Pad

25 ⊗31

The Walk at JBR

Dhow Cruise

Jumeirah Lakes Towers Pier 7

12 18 Residence 1

37 ⊙1

Jumeirah Beach Residence 1

36

Murjan Ave

21 ⊗

23

13

Skydive Dubai

Jungle Bay Waterpark

11

26 10

Club Mina

One&Only Spa

29

14 ⊙

Palm West Beach ⊙9

17 20 ⊗

24 ⊗

Palm Jumeirah

King Salman Bin Abdulaziz Al Saud St

Knowledge Village

Al Sufouh

DUBAI MEDIA CITY

Dubai Media City

DUBAI INTERNET CITY

Palm Jumeirah

King Salman Bin Abdulaziz Al Saud St

Dubai Internet City Ⓜ

BARSHA HEIGHTS

28

27

30

33

19 ⊗

Mina Al Seyahi

Marina Towers

Marina Ⓜ

Sheikh Zayed Rd

King Salman Bin Abdulaziz Al Saud St

Interchange No 5

Dubai Marina Ⓜ

22 ⊗

Sobha Realty Ⓜ

Al Khail Ⓜ

Emirates Golf Club

16 ⊙ Emirates Golf Club

Dubai Marina Mall

DMCC Ⓜ

Jumeirah Lakes Towers Ⓜ

JUMEIRAH LAKES TOWERS

38

5 6 7 8

A B C D E F

Sights

The Walk at JBR

AREA

1 ⊙ MAP P126, B6

In a city of air-conditioned malls, this attractive outdoor shopping and dining promenade was an immediate hit when it opened in 2008, originally to meet the needs of the 20,000 people living in the Jumeirah Beach Residence development. Today The Walk is also a big hit with tourists who join locals in strolling the 1.7km stretch, watching the world on parade from a pavement cafe, browsing the fashionable boutiques or ogling the shiny Ferraris (and other fancy cars) cruising by on weekends. (Jumeirah Beach Residence, Dubai Marina; ⓜDMCC, ⏭Jumeirah Beach Residence 1, Jumeirah Beach Residence 2)

The Beach at JBR

AREA

2 ⊙ MAP P126, A6

Paralleling the beachfront for about 1km, The Beach at JBR is an open-plan cluster of low-lying, urban-style buildings wrapped around breezy plazas. Hugely popular with families on weekends, it mixes cafes and upmarket shops with a lively waterfront fun zone complete with a kiddie splash park, an outdoor gym, a crafts market and other diversions. A beach club rents out sunloungers, or you can spread your towel just about anywhere for free. (☏04 317 3999; www.thebeach.ae; Jumeirah Beach Residence, Dubai Marina; ⏰10am-midnight Sun-Wed, to 1am Thu-Sat; Ⓟ�person; ⓜDMCC, ⏭Jumeirah Beach Residence 1, Jumeirah Beach Residence 2)

Ain Dubai

FERRIS WHEEL

3 ⊙ MAP P126, A5

Size always matters in Dubai, so it's no surprise that Ain Dubai sets the record for world's largest observation wheel. Standing a vertigo-inducing 250m tall, it's almost twice the height of the London Eye. Riding in one of the 48 high-tech pods gives you 38 minutes to gawk at the urban skyline, Palm Jumeirah and the Gulf. If the views don't make you giddy enough, opt for a party cabin complete with music and 'sky bar'.

Private cabins and other packages are also available. Open since 2021, Ain Dubai is the centrepiece of the artificial Bluewaters Island which juts out from the JBR shoreline and is peppered with the usual mix of restaurants, hotels and residences as well as the local version of Madame Tussauds wax museum. The nicest way to get to the island is on the 20-minute boat ride from the Dubai Marina Mall (Dhs5). (Dubai Eye; ☏800 246 392; www.aindubai.com; Bluewaters Island, Dubai Marina; adult/child from Dhs130/100; ⏰10am-9pm Tue & Wed, noon-9pm Thu-Sat; 🚢Bluewaters Marine Transport Station, ⓜDMCC, ⏭Jumeirah Beach Residence 2)

IR STONE/SHUTTERSTOCK ©

Aquaventure Waterpark

Aquaventure Waterpark
WATER PARK

4 ◉ MAP P126, E1

Adrenalin rushes are guaranteed at this water park at the Atlantis The Palm resort. A 1.6km-long 'river' with rapids, wave surges and waterfalls meanders through vast grounds that are anchored by two towers. A highlight is the ziggurat-shaped Tower of Neptune, with three slides, including the aptly named Leap of Faith, a near-vertical plunge into a shark-infested lagoon. (☎04 426 1169; www.atlantisthepalm.com; Atlantis The Palm, Palm Jumeirah; over/under 120cm tall Dhs275/230; ⏰10am-sunset; 👶; 🚇Palm Jumeirah, 🚊Atlantis Aquaventure)

Lost Chambers Aquarium
AQUARIUM

5 ◉ MAP P126, E1

Rare albino alligators Ali and Blue are the latest stars in this fantastic labyrinth of underwater halls, enclosures and fish tanks that re-creates the legend of the lost city of Atlantis. Some 65,000 exotic marine creatures inhabit 21 aquariums, where rays flutter, jellyfish dance and giant groupers lurk. The centrepiece is the Ambassador Lagoon. For an extra fee, you can snorkel or dive with the fishes in this 11.5-million-litre tank. (☎04 426 1040; www.atlantisthepalm.com; Atlantis The Palm, Palm Jumeirah; adult/child 3-11yr Dhs125/90; ⏰10am-10pm; 🅿; 🚇Palm Jumeirah, 🚊Atlantis Aquaventure)

Nostalgic Cruise Trips

Local company **Tour Dubai** (Map p126, B7; 04 336 8407; www.tour-dubai.com; Tour Dubai, Marina Walk, below Al Gharbi St bridge, Dubai Marina; 1hr tour adult/child Dhs50/40, dinner cruises Dhs250/125; Ⓜ DMCC, Ⓡ Dubai Marina Mall) runs guided one-hour boat tours with prerecorded English commentary aboard nostalgic dhows outfitted with colourful upholstered benches. There are eight tours daily between 10.30am and 5.30pm. In the evening, the dhows set sail for a two-hour dinner buffet with taped music. Alcohol is available.

JBR Beach   BEACH

6 MAP P126, A6

This clean, wonderful playground has plenty of facilities, including showers, toilets and changing rooms housed in distinctive panelled pods. Kids can keep cool in a splash zone, and there's even an outdoor gym for pumping iron. Since it's right next to The Beach at JBR (p128) and The Walk at JBR (p128), there's no shortage of food and drink outlets, although alcohol is only available in the hotels. (Jumeirah Beach Residence, Dubai Marina; ♿; Ⓜ DMCC, Ⓡ Jumeirah Beach Residence 1)

Fairmont The Palm Beach Club   BEACH

7 MAP P126, E4

Views of the mainland skyline are one of the most memorable aspects of a day at this family-orientated club at the swish Fairmont Hotel. Parents get to wriggle their toes in the sand or by the pool while the little ones let off steam in the Fairmont Falcon Juniors' Club. (📞 04 457 3388; www.fairmont.com/palm-dubai; Fairmont The Palm, Palm Jumeirah; day pass weekday/weekend adult Dhs250/300, child Dhs150; ⏱ 6.30am-8pm; 🅿 ♿; Ⓜ Nakheel, Ⓡ Palm Jumeirah)

The View at The Palm   VIEWPOINT

8 ◎ MAP P126, E4

For a chance to marvel at Palm Jumeirah's impressive outline without hopping on an airplane, head to this outdoor viewing deck perched at a lofty 240m on the 52nd floor of the Palm Tower. Tickets also include a spin around digitally enhanced exhibits detailing the creation of this vast island archipelago. Various upgrades, including fast-track tickets and lounge access, are available. The entrance is from Nakheel Mall.

Record chasers should buy a pass to The Next Level, one floor above and only 10m higher but therefore the highest vantage point on Palm Jumeirah. (📞 800 843 8439; www.theviewpalm.ae; Center of Palm; adult/child from Dhs100/69;

⏱9am-10pm Mon-Thu, to midnight Fri-Sun, last entry 1hr before closing; 𝐏; 🚇Nakheel Mall)

Palm West Beach   BEACH

9 ⊙ MAP P126, D5

Hemming in a west-facing 1.6-km section along Palm Jumeirah's trunk, this restaurant-, bar- and hotel-lined promenade and beach make for a dreamy spot to watch the sun plop below the horizon, toes in sand and cold drink in hand. For upscale socialising, book a lounger in a luxe club like Beach by Five, famous for its glass-fronted swimming pool. (☎800 625 4335; www.westbeach.ae; Palm Jumeirah; ⏱8am-midnight Mon-Fri, to 3am Sat-Sun; 🚇Al Ittihad Park)

Club Mina   BEACH

10 ⊙ MAP P126, D6

Set along 500m of private beach, this club is a family favourite thanks to its five pools (including a shaded one for kids), a children's club and a water-sports centre. Nice touch for grown-ups: cocktails in the swim-up bar. Children get free admission on

Tuesdays. (☎04 399 3333; www.clubminadubai.com; Le Méridien Mina Seyahi Beach Resort, King Salman Bin Abdulaziz Al Saud St, Dubai Media City; day pass weekday/weekend adult Dhs220/310, child Dhs110/160; 𝐏🚸; 🚇Nahkeel)

Jungle Bay Waterpark   WATER PARK

11 ⊙ MAP P126, C6

Attractively designed in Greece-inspired blue and white around a jaunty lighthouse, this small water park sits just steps from the beach at Le Méridien Mina Seyahi resort and delivers aquatic fun for all ages. Race your friends on the side-by-side Whizzard Slides, float in the wave pool or watch your little ones get wet safely in the AquaPlay area.

Admission is free for hotel guests. (☎04 399 3333; www.marriott.com/en-us/hotels/dxbms-le-meridien-mina-seyahi-beach-resort-and-waterpark/experiences/; King Salman Bin Adult Aziz Al Saud St; adult/child Dhs200/100 weekdays, Dhs300/200 weekends; ⏱9am-5pm or later daily; 🚸; 🚇Al Khail, 🚇Mina Seyahi)

Riding the Dubai Tram

The Dubai Marina is one of the most pedestrian-friendly areas in town and is also served by the Dubai Tram (www.alsufouhtram.com), which makes 11 stops, including one near the Marina Mall, The Beach at JBR and The Walk at JBR. It also connects with the Sobha Realty and DMCC metro stations and with the Palm Jumeirah Monorail at Palm Jumeirah station. Nol Cards must be used.

Dubai Marina & Palm Jumeirah Sights

Desert Explorations

For travellers on short trips to Dubai, an organised 4WD desert safari is the most popular way to experience the Arabian sands. Typical tours involve off-roading, camel riding, henna painting and belly dancing, followed by a Middle Eastern dinner. Cheaper tours head for Al Awir, 35km east of Downtown, while a few companies, including **Platinum Heritage Tours** (📞04 388 4044; www.platinum-heritage.com; 3rd fl, Oasis Centre, Sheikh Zayed Rd, Al Quoz 1; ⊙office hours 8am-6pm; Ⓜ Al Safa, Umm Al Seef) and **Arabian Adventures** (📞04 303 4888, 800 272 2426; www.arabian-adventures.com; Sheikh Zayed Rd, Emirates Holiday Bldg; Sundowner Dinner Safari Dhs250; ⊙10am-10pm), are permitted to take travellers into the Dubai Desert Conservation Reserve for a more genuine, sustainable experience.

Pier 7
NOTABLE BUILDING

12 ◎ MAP P126, B7

Linked to the Dubai Marina Mall via a glass-encased walkway, this circular tower gets its name from the seven restaurants on each of its floors. All but the lowest one have terrace tables for noshing with a view. (📞04 436 1020; www.pier7.ae; Marina Walk, Dubai Marina; Ⓟ; Ⓜ Sobha Realty, 🚇Dubai Marina Mall)

Skydive Dubai
SKYDIVING

13 ◎ MAP P126, C6

Daredevils can experience the rush of jumping out of a plane and see-ing Palm Jumeirah and the Dubai skyline from the air by signing up for these tandem parachute flights. The minimum age is 18; weight and height restrictions apply. (📞04 377 8888; www.skydivedubai.ae; Al Seyahi St, Dubai Marina; tandem jump, video & photos Dhs2199; ⊙8am-4pm Mon-Sat; Ⓜ Sobha Realty)

One&Only Spa
SPA

14 ◎ MAP P126, D6

Do you want to unwind, restore or elevate? These are the magic words at this exclusive spa with a dozen treatment rooms where massages, wraps, scrubs and facials are calibrated to achieve your chosen goal. Or opt for a session in the Oriental Hammam with its soothing meditative music, Moroccan decor and hot stone massage. (📞04 315 2140; www.royalmirage.oneandonlyresorts.com; One&Only Royal Mirage, King Salman Bin Abdulaziz Al Saud St, Dubai Media City; ⊙9.30am-9pm (women only until 1pm); Ⓜ Al Khail)

Splash Pad
WATER PARK

15 ◎ MAP P126, A6

Younger children can keep cool in the fountains, sprinklers, tipping buckets and other watery fun spots at this cheerfully coloured mini water park right next to the sand. The fenced-in area also includes a dry-play area with swings, see-saws and climbing frames. (www.thebeach.ae/en/play/splash-pad; The Beach at JBR, Dubai Marina; per hour/day Dhs65/99; ⏰9am-8pm; 🚹; Ⓜ D-MCC, 🚊Jumeirah Beach Residence 2)

Emirates Golf Club   GOLF

16 ◎ MAP P126, D8

This prestigious club has two courses: the flagship international championship Majlis course, which hosts the annual **Dubai Desert Classic** (📞04 383 3588; www.omegadubaidesertclassic.com; Emirates Golf Club, Emirates Hills 2; tickets Dhs75-175; ⏰Feb; 📶; Ⓜ Nakheel), and the Faldo course, which is the only floodlit 18-hole course in the country. Beginners can go wild

on the par-three nine-hole course (peak/off-peak Dhs130/95). (📞04 417 9800, 04 380 1234; www.dubaigolf.com; Interchange No 5, Sheikh Zayed Rd, Emirates Hills 2; Majlis/Faldo Mon-Fri Dhs995/595, Sat & Sun Dhs1200/695; Ⓜ Al Khail)

Eating

Stay   FRENCH $$$

17 🍴 MAP P126, C5

Three-Michelin-starred Yannick Alléno brings his culinary magic to Dubai in this subtly theatrical vaulted dining room accented with black crystal chandeliers. His creations seem deceptively simple (the beef tenderloin with fries and black pepper sauce is a bestseller), letting the superb ingredients shine brightly. An unexpected stunner is

Skydive Dubai

VIKTORKOZLOV/SHUTTERSTOCK ©

Dubai Marina & Palm Jumeirah Eating

the Pastry Library, an entire wall of sweet treats. (☎04 440 1030; www.thepalm.oneandonlyresorts.com; One&Only The Palm, West Crescent, Palm Jumeirah; mains Dhs190-290; ⏱7-11pm Tue-Sun; 🅿🛜; Ⓜ Sobha Realty, 🚋Palm Jumeirah)

Asia Asia   FUSION $$$

18 🔀 MAP P126, B7

Prepare for a culinary journey along the Spice Road at this theatrically decorated restaurant, which is entered via a candlelit corridor that spills into an exotic booth-lined lounge with dangling birdcage lamps. Dim sum to tuna tataki and crispy duck – dishes here are alive with flavours from Asia and the Middle East. Bonus: the grand marina views from the terrace. Full bar. (☎04 276 5900; www.asia-asia.com; 6th fl, Pier 7, Dubai Marina; mains Dhs85-350; ⏱4pm-midnight; 🛜; Ⓜ Sobha Realty, 🚋Dubai Marina Mall)

Indego by Vineet   INDIAN $$$

19 🔀 MAP P126, C6

India's first Michelin-starred chef, Vineet Bhatia, is the menu maven at this gorgeous, intimate dining room lorded over by big brass Natraj sculptures. Dishes straddle the line between tradition and innovation; in the former category, the butter chicken and *rasmalai* (cardamom-spiced creamy dessert) are particularly outstanding. (☎04 317 6000; www.indegobyvineet.com; ground fl, Tower One, Grosvenor House, Al Emreef St, Dubai Marina;

mains Dhs115-240; ⏱7pm-midnight; 🅿🛜; Ⓜ Sobha Realty, 🚋Jumeirah Beach Residence 1)

101 Lounge & Bar   SEAFOOD $$$

20 🔀 MAP P126, C5

It may be hard to concentrate on the food at this marina-adjacent al fresco pavilion, with its stunning skyline views. Come for nibbles and cocktails in the bar or go for the full dinner experience, with seafood the star attraction. Be sure to check out the ultraswish Champagne Bar. Note that there is a smart-casual dress code after 6.30pm. (☎04 440 1010; www.thepalm.oneandonlyresorts.com; One&Only The Palm, West Crescent, Palm Jumeirah; mains Dhs105-295; ⏱11.30am-2am Mon-Sat; 🛜; Ⓜ Sobha Realty, 🚋Palm Jumeirah)

Maya Modern
Mexican Kitchen   MEXICAN $$$

21 🔀 MAP P126, C6

Richard Sandoval, the man who introduced modern Mexican food to the US, is behind the menu at this casual-chic restaurant with its contemporary take on rural Mexican dishes. The result is a piñata of flavours, from creamy guacamole (prepared tableside) to fish tacos with peanut sauce and chicken *mole poblano* to sizzling prawn fajitas.(☎04 316 5550; www.maya-dubai.com; Le Royal Meridien Beach Resort & Spa, Al Mamsha St, Dubai Marina; mains Dhs100-200; ⏱7pm-1am Mon-Sat; 🅿🛜; Ⓜ Sobha Realty, 🚋Jumeirah Beach Residence 1)

Women in the UAE

Some of the biggest misunderstandings between Middle Easterners and people from other parts of the world occur over the issue of women.

Common Misconceptions

Half-truths and stereotypes exist on both sides: foreigners sometimes assume that all Middle Eastern women are veiled, repressed victims, while some locals see Western women as sex-obsessed and immoral. Many non-Arab people imagine that for women to travel to Dubai is much more difficult and stressful than it is. First up, let's clear up some common myths: You don't have to wear a burka, headscarf or veil. You are allowed to drive a car. You won't be constantly harassed. It's safe to take taxis, stay alone in hotels and walk around on your own in most areas.

Emirati Women in Society

Traditionally, the role of a woman in this region is to be a mother and matron of the household, while the man is the financial provider. However, the reality is far more nuanced. Emirati women in the UAE pilot planes, work as police officers, undertake research and run corporations. Seven of 29 members of the UAE cabinet are women.

Marriage

A Muslim man is permitted by Islam to have up to four wives (but a woman may have only one husband). This practice within Islam originally came about due to practical considerations: the ability of a man to take more than one wife enabled men to marry women who had been widowed (and thus left without a provider).

Today, most Emiratis have only one wife, however, not least because Islam dictates that each spouse must be loved and treated equally. Besides, housing and child rearing are expensive – perhaps a reason why the average number of children in modern Emirati families has declined from five to two.

Mythos Kouzina & Grill

GREEK $$

22 MAP P126, B7

Kitted out like a traditional seaside taverna with whitewashed walls and sea-green painted furniture, Mythos is a little slice of Santorini hidden away in the somewhat incongruous setting of JLT's Armada BlueBay Hotel. Order a selection of starters to share – the *keftedakia* (meatballs) are particularly good – and then it's a toss-up between home-style favourites such as moussaka and souvlaki and succulent grilled meats and seafood. (☏04 399 8166; www.mythoskouzina.com; level B1, Armada BlueBay Hotel, Cluster P, Jumeirah Lakes Towers; mains Dhs45-89; ⏱12.30-5pm & 7-11.30pm; P 🛜; MSobha Realty)

Zero Gravity
INTERNATIONAL $$

23 ✕ MAP P126, C6

Next to the Skydive Dubai drop zone, this stylish outpost with attached beach club checks all the culinary boxes, from breakfast to late-night snacks. Pizza, pasta, sandwiches, grills and salads are all fresh, healthy and perfectly pitched to mainstream tastes. After dark, the party people descend and the place revs up the tempo with dancing and a resident DJ. (☏04 399 0009; www.0-gravity.ae; Al Seyahi St, Skydive Dubai Drop Zone, Dubai Marina; mains Dhs50-250; ⏱8am-2am; P 🛜; MDamac)

Eauzone
ASIAN $$$

24 ✕ MAP P126, E6

This jewel of a restaurant draws friends, romancing couples and fashionable families to a sublime seaside setting with shaded wooden decks and floating *majlis* (reception room) overlooking illuminated pools. Casual by day, it's hushed and intimate at night, perfect for concentrating on such pleasurable Asian classics as lotus-wrapped sea bass or miso-glazed black cod. (☏04 399 9999; www.royalmirage.oneandonly

Mezze (selection of hot and cold dishes)

XAVIERARNAU/GETTY IMAGES ©

resorts.com; Arabian Court, One&Only Royal Mirage, King Salman Bin Abdulaziz Al Saud St, Dubai Media City; mains Dhs80-165; ⏱noon-3.30pm & 7-11.30pm; 🅿 🛜; Ⓜ Al Khail, 🚋Palm Jumeirah)

BiCE

ITALIAN $$$

25 MAP P126, B6

Back in 1930s Milan, Beatrice 'Bice' Ruggeri first opened her trattoria, which evolved into the city's most fashionable by the 1970s. Today Dubai's BiCE carries on the tradition, with chef Davide Gardini adding his creative touch to such classics as fettuccine with lobster and veal tenderloin with foie gras sauce. Nice touch: the olive-oil trolley. (☎04 399 1111; www. bicemare.com; Hilton Dubai Jumeirah, The Walk at JBR, Dubai Marina; pasta Dhs70-195, mains Dhs150-230; ⏱12.30-3.30pm & 7-11.30pm; 🅿 🛜; Ⓜ DMCC, 🚋Jumeirah Beach Residence 1)

Drinking

Barasti

BAR

26 🚇 MAP P126, C6

Since 1995, Barasti has grown from basic beach shack to top beach club spot for lazy days in the sand, and is often jam-packed with shiny happy party people knocking back the brewskis. There's football and rugby on the big screen, plus pool tables (and pool parties), water-sports rentals, a daily happy hour, occasional bands and drink specials on most weeknights. (☎04 318 1313; www. barastibeach.com; King Salman Bin Abdulaziz Al Saud St, Dubai Media City; ⏱9am-2am Sun-Thu, to 3am Fri & Sat; 🛜; Ⓜ Al Khail)

Lock, Stock & Barrel

BAR

27 🚇 MAP P126, F8

Since opening in 2016, LSB has been racking up the accolades as living proof that there's room in bling-blinded Dubai for keeping-it-real party hangouts. Dressed in industrial chic, this two-level joint is the place for mingling with unpretentious folk over cocktails and craft beer, twice-weekly live bands and fingerlickin' American soul food. Two-for-one happy hour daily from 4pm to 8pm. (☎04 514 9195; www.lsbdubai.com; 8th fl, Grand Millennium Hotel, Barsha Heights; ⏱4pm-3am Mon-Thu, from 1pm Fri, from 2pm Sat & Sun)

Lucky Voice

KARAOKE

28 🚇 MAP P126, F8

This UK import features private karaoke pods where groups of six to 25 people can belt out tunes from a huge playlist without (much) fear of embarrassment. Even if you're not into singing, come for ladies' nights, Saturday brunch or on nights when the house band plays highly danceable funk, rock and soul classics. (☎800 58259; www. luckyvoice.ae; Grand Millennium Hotel, Barsha Heights; 2hr incl drinks Dhs150; ⏱2pm-3am Mon-Thu, from 1pm Fri, 5pm-3am Sat & Sun; 🛜; Ⓜ Dubai Internet City)

Jetty Lounge BAR

29 ☕ MAP P126, D6

From the moment you start following the meandering path through One&Only's luxuriant gardens, you'll sense that you're heading for a pretty special place. Classy without the pretence, Jetty Lounge is all about unwinding (preferably at sunset) on plush white sofas scattered right in the sand. There's a full bar menu and global snacks. (📞04 399 9999; www.royalmirage.oneandonly resorts.com; One&Only Royal Mirage, The Palace, King Salman Bin Abdulaziz Al Saud St, Dubai Media City; ⏰2pm-2am; 📶; Ⓜ Al Khail, 🚋Media City)

Siddharta Lounge BAR

30 ☕ MAP P126, C6

Part of Buddha Bar in the same hotel, Siddharta is an urban oasis and great spot to join Dubai's glam crowd in taking the party from daytime by the pool to basking in the glow of the Marina high-rises at night. Nice music, expertly mixed cocktails and swift service make up for the rather steep price tab. (📞04 317 6000; www. siddhartalounge.com; Tower 2, Grosvenor House, Al Emreef St, Al Saud St, Dubai Marina; ⏰12.30-3.30pm & 5pm-midnight Sun-Thu, to 1am Fri, 7pm-1am Sat; 📶; Ⓜ Sobha Realty)

Pure Sky Lounge BAR

31 ☕ MAP P126, B6

When it comes to glorious views over The Beach at JBR and Palm Jumeirah, this chic indoor-outdoor lounge is in a lofty league on the 35th floor of the beachfront Hilton. White furniture accented with turquoise pillows channels a chill, maritime mood. (📞04 399 1111; www3.hilton.com; Hilton Dubai Jumeirah, The Walk at JBR, Dubai Marina; ⏰5pm-1am; 📶; Ⓜ Sobha Realty, 🚋Jumeirah Beach Residence 1)

Bliss Lounge BAR

32 ☕ MAP P126, A6

Sunset is the perfect time to stake out your turf at the circular bar or on a cushiony sofa in a tented 'pod' at this beachfront lounge with view of the Ain Dubai Ferris wheel. Kick back with a cold one or a shisha while nibbling on sushi and taking in some tunes courtesy of a resident DJ. Service can be hit or miss. (📞04 315 3886; www.bliss loungedubai.com; Sheraton Jumeirah Beach Resort, Al Mamsha St, The Walk at JBR, Dubai Marina; ⏰12.30pm-2am; 📶; Ⓜ DMCC)

Buddha Bar BAR

33 ☕ MAP P126, C6

If there are celebs in town, they'll show up at Buddha Bar to enjoy superbly handcrafted cocktails surrounded by a dramatic Asian-inspired interior decked out with gorgeous chandeliers, a wall of reflective sheer glass and an enormous Buddha lording over the heathens. (📞04 317 6000; www. buddhabar-dubai.com; Grosvenor House, Al Emreef St, Dubai Marina; ⏰7pm-1am Sun-Fri, 8pm-2am Sat; 📶; Ⓜ Sobha Realty, 🚋Dubai Marina Mall)

Entertainment

MusicHall
LIVE MUSIC

34 ⭐ MAP P126, C4

It's not a theatre, not a club, not a bar and not a restaurant – the lavishly designed MusicHall is all those things. The concept hails from Beirut, where it's had audiences clapping since 2003 with an eclectic line-up of 10 live-music acts – from Indian to country, and rock to Russian ballads. The food (fusion cuisine and international finger food) is an afterthought. There's a minimum spend of Dhs450. (📞056 270 8670; www. themusichall.com; ground fl, Jumeirah Zabeel Saray, West Crescent, Palm Jumeirah; ⏰9pm-3am Fri & Sat; Ⓜ Sobha Realty, 🚋 Palm Jumeirah)

Shopping

Nakheel Mall
MALL

35 🔒 MAP P126, E4

With 300 shops, this snazzy new mall on the trunk of Palm Jumeirah may not be Dubai's biggest shopping emporium but it does count a rooftop lounge-bar, a Vox cinema and a trampoline park among its distinctive assets. It also provides access to The View at The Palm (p131) and Aura, a 360-degree infinity pool lounge suspended 200 metres in the air. (📞800 625 4335; www.nakheelmall.ae; Center of Palm, Palm Jumeirah; ⏰10am-10pm Mon-Thu, to midnight Fri-Sun; 🚋 Nakheel Mall)

Dubai Marina Mall
MALL

36 🔒 MAP P126, B7

This mall has an attractive water-front setting and a manageable 140 stores on four floors, so you won't get lost quite so readily as in its mega-size cousins. Its main architectural feature is the giant atrium where kids can trundle around in a toy train. (📞04 436 1020; www.dubaimarinamall.com; Dubai Marina Walk, Dubai Marina; ⏰10am-10pm Sun-Thu, to 11pm Fri & Sat; 📶👫; Ⓜ Sobha Realty, 🚋 Dubai Marina Mall)

Gallery One
ART

37 🔒 MAP P126, B6

If you love art but can't afford an original, pick up a highly decorative print by well-known Middle Eastern artists without breaking the bank at this gallery shop. Some motifs are also available as greetings cards, posters, notebooks and calendars. (📞04 423 1987; www.g-1. com; The Walk at JBR, Dubai Marina; ⏰10am-10pm; Ⓜ DMCC, 🚋 Jumeirah Beach Residence 1)

Ibn Battuta Mall
MALL

38 🔒 MAP P126, A7

The lavish and exotic design and architecture of this 400-shop mall steals the show, tracing the way stations of 14th-century Moroccan explorer Ibn Battuta in six themed courts.(📞04 390 9999; www.ibn battutamall.com; Sheikh Zayed Rd, btwn Interchanges No 5 & No 6, Jebel Ali; ⏰10am-10pm; Ⓜ Ibn Battuta)

Dubai Experience 🍽️

Let's Do Brunch

Saturday brunch is a major element of the Dubai social scene and just about every hotel-restaurant in town sets up an all-you-can-eat buffet with an option for unlimited wine or bubbly. Here are our top indulgence picks in town. Reservations essential.

Brunch Tips

○ Make Saturday brunch reservations at least a week ahead.

○ Head out early – trying to find a taxi and battling the traffic at 12.30pm is not fun.

❶ The Motherlode

Expect to loosen your belt after enjoying the cornucopia of delectables at the Saturday Brunch at **Al Qasr** (www.jumeirah.com; Ⓜ Mall of the Emirates). Options include barbecued Wagyu burgers and global treats from Bangkok, Paris and Mexico. A live band provides entertainment. Brunch with soft drinks/alcohol costs Dhs495/595.

❷ Spice Route Brunch

The food is as sumptuous as the decor at **Asia Asia** (p134) restaurant with terrace tables overlooking the Dubai Marina. Work your way from raw bar to the sushi selection, then feast on crab cakes before hitting the slow roasted lamb or miso-marinated salmon. Held from 2pm to 5pm on Saturdays, brunch costs Dhs350 with drinks.

❸ Jazz Brunch

The cheap and cheerful brunch at **Jazz@PizzaExpress** (www.pizzaexpressuae.com; Ⓜ DMCC) has you filling up on Italian faves – antipasti, pasta, thin-crust pizza – ordered à la carte and brought to your table. Live jazz sets the mood. Brunch with/without alcohol costs Dhs199/129.

❹ International Indulgence

Bubbalicious (www.westinmina seyahi.com; Ⓜ Al Khail) is the culinary bonanza orchestrated at the Westin Dubai Mina Seyahi Beach Resort & Marina. It features everything from oysters to cheesecake, plus 10 live cooking stations and family-friendly entertainment such as a petting zoo and a play area. Brunch with soft drinks/sparkling wine costs Dhs450/550.

❺ Afternoon Revelry

Perfect for sleepyheads, the Onshore Social at the **Zero Gravity** (p136) beach club kicks into gear in the afternoon amid an avalanche of global faves, from dim sum to antipasti and lamb chops to decadent desserts. Stay on for sunset and night-time DJ beats. Brunch costs Dhs395, but if you want sparkling wine and pool and beach access, it's bumped up to Dhs666.

❻ Fiesta Time

At the Mas Mas Maya brunch by the beach at **Maya Modern Mexican Kitchen** (p134), you can fuel up on fajitas, guacamole and ceviche before capping it off with churros and ice cream. Includes pool and beach access to the Royal Meridien Beach Resort & Spa. Brunch is 12.30pm to 4pm on Saturdays and costs Dhs325/Dhs475 with soft drinks/alcohol.

❼ Carnivorous Delight

Fans of churrasco grills will be in heaven at the Hola Hola brunch at **Toro Toro** (www.torotoro-dubai.com; Ⓜ Sobha Realty). Offering the regular menu's most popular dishes, this brunch is a great way to sample celebrity chef Richard Sandoval's culinary concoctions. Brunch starts from Dhs300.

Worth a Trip 🔭
Explore Art and Culture in Abu Dhabi

The first Louvre outside France, an ethereally beautiful mosque, the world's fastest roller coaster, a head-spinning Formula One racetrack. About 150km south of Dubai, the UAE capital Abu Dhabi may not be quite as flashy as its northern cousin but – almost stealthily – it too has built up an impressive portfolio of attractions and sharpened its profile as a popular tourist destination of its own. Welcome to an exciting city where nothing stands still.

Abu Dhabi is a simple day trip from Dubai, easily manageable on public transport or by yourself.

🚌 Every 40 minutes from Dubai's Al Gubaiba station in Bur Dubai (single/return Dhs25/40, two hours)

🚕 Taxis cost around Dhs300.

Louvre Abu Dhabi

In the stunning Jean Nouvel–designed **Louvre Abu Dhabi** (www.louvreabudhabi.ae; Saadiyat Island; adult/aged 13-22yr/under 13yr Dhs63/31/free), sunlight filters through its huge perforated dome onto a cluster of 23 galleries sheltering 600 priceless works that illustrate our shared humanity across time, ethnicity and geography. Highlights include a Da Vinci painting, a Chinese Buddha and a bronze from Benin.

Sheikh Zayed Grand Mosque

Rising majestically from beautifully manicured gardens, the **Sheikh Zayed Grand Mosque** (www.szgmc.ae; off Sheikh Rashid Bin Saeed St; admission free; ⏱9am-10pm Sat-Thu, 4.30-10pm Fri, tours 10am, 11am & 5pm Sun-Thu, 5pm & 7pm Fri, 10am, 11am, 2pm, 5pm & 7pm Sat) represents an impressive welcome to the city. It accommodates 50,000 worshippers and is one of the few in the region open to non-Muslims.

Emirates Palace

What the Burj Khalifa in Dubai is to the vertical, the **Emirates Palace** (www.emiratespalace.com; Corniche Rd (West); admission free; pictured) is to the horizontal, with audacious domed gatehouses and flying ramps to the foyer, 114 domes and a 1.3km private beach. Built for Dhs11 billion, this is the big hotel in the Gulf, with 1002 crystal chandeliers and 392 luxury rooms and suites.

Abu Dhabi Falcon Hospital

Falcons are an integral part of traditional Gulf culture, which is what makes this **facility** (www.falconhospital.com; Sweihan Rd; 2hr tour adult/child Dhs170/60; ⏱tours 10am & 2pm Mon-Thu, 10am Fri & Sun) much-needed and much-loved. Tours include visits to the falcon museum, the examination room and the free-flight aviary. Reservations required.

★ **Top Tips**

o To get your bearings, consider a trip on the hop-on, hop-off **Big Bus Abu Dhabi** (📞02 449 0026; www.bigbustours.com; 24hr adult/child Dhs260/166; ⏱9am-5pm).

o Take a free guided tour of the Grand Mosque, which includes a Q&A (in English).

✕ **Take a Break**

Al Dhafra (www.aldhafrauae.ae; Al Mina Port; buffet lunch/dinner from Dhs120/99, dinner cruise Dhs150; ⏱noon-5pm & 6.30-11.15pm; 📱) is a hidden Arab gem serving the best Emirati cuisine in town.

For the ultimate indulgence, order a cappuccino sprinkled with 24-karat gold flakes (Dhs60) at **Le Café** (www.emiratespalace.com; Corniche Rd (West), Emirates Palace; high tea for 2 people Dhs387-478; ⏱6.30am-1am, high tea 2-6pm; 📱) in the Emirates Palace.

Survival Guide

Camel resting on desert sand dunes IVAN KURMYSHOV/SHUTTERSTOCK ©

Before You Go

Book Your Stay

o Room rates fluctuate enormously, spiking during festivals, holidays and big events and dropping in the summer months.

o A 10% municipal tax, 10% service fee, 5% VAT and a 'tourism tax' ranging from Dh7 to Dh20 per night are added to room rates.

o Even midrange hotels often have superb facilities, including a pool, restaurants, a gym, satellite TV and a bar.

o Not all hotels are licensed to serve alcohol, so check if this is important to you.

o Hotel apartments are great for self-caterers, families and groups.

o Nostalgic types should check into the growing crop of heritage boutique hotels in Bur Dubai and Deira.

o By law, unmarried men and women are not permitted to share a room, but it is not enforced in reality.

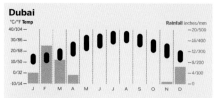

Dubai

°C/°F Temp — Rainfall inches/mm

When to Go

o **Winter** (Dec–Feb) Moderate temperatures, short days, occasional rain, many festivals and activities.

o **Spring** (Mar–Apr) Perfect beach weather with temperatures around 30°C.

o **Summer** (Jul–Sep) Temperatures soar (to an average 43°C with stifling 95% humidity), hotel rates drop.

o **Autumn** (Oct–Nov) Warm weather, balmy nights, life moves back outdoors.

o Free wi-fi is commonplace, with only a few hotels charging as much Dhs100 per day for access.

Useful Websites

Lonely Planet (www. lonelyplanet.com/ united-arab-emirates/ dubai/hotels) Recommendations and bookings.

Visit Dubai (www.visit dubai.com) The official tourist authority site also has accommodation booking function.

Dnata (www.dnata travel.com) Major travel agency for the Middle Eastern market, based in Dubai.

Best Budget

Rove Downtown (www.rovehotels.com) Budget-friendly urban base with Burj Khalifa views.

Ibis Mall of the Emirates (www.ibis. com) Predictably basic but comfortable and in a primo location.

Premier Inn Dubai International Airport (https://global. premierinn.com) Easy in, easy out at this airport-adjacent budget designer hotel.

Rove City Centre (www.rovehotels.com) Hip yet down-to-earth with amenities that are more typical of posher players.

Centro Barsha (www.rotana.com/centrobarsha) Designer hotel with key lifestyle and tech touches near Mall of the Emirates.

Best Midrange

XVA Hotel (www.xvahotel.com) Connect to the magic of a bygone era in this art-filled heritage den.

Le Meridien Mina Seyahi Beach Resort (www.lemeridienminaseyahi.com) Good-value waterfront outpost for sporty types.

Media One Hotel (www.mediaonehotel.com) High-octane hot spot with mod design, party pedigree and unpretentious attitude.

Pearl Marina Hotel Apartments (www.pearlmarinahotel.com) All the charms of Dubai Marina at your feet at a good price.

Beach Hotel Apartment (http://beachhotelapartment.ae) Rare bargain in Jumeirah with a killer location and easy access to tanning and shopping.

Best Top End

Al Qasr Hotel (www.jumeirah.com) Posh player with A-lister clientele, 2km of private beach and canalside dining.

Grosvenor House (www.grosvenorhouse-dubai.com) Art deco–inspired hotel draws local trend-chasers to its hip bars and restaurants.

One&Only The Palm (http://thepalm.oneandonlyresorts.com) Sumptuous resort with Moorish-style design accents, lavish Arabian-style and expansive gardens.

Park Hyatt Dubai Class act surrounded by lush landscaping with superb facilities and golf course access.

Raffles Dubai (www.raffles.com/dubai) Slick, chic decor with water features and top-rated Japanese rooftop restaurant and lounge.

Palace Downtown (www.theaddress.com) Romantic inner-city pad with easy access to top shopping and dreamy views of Burj Khalifa.

Arriving in Dubai

Dubai International Airport

○ Most international flights land at this airport north of Deira.

○ Dubai metro's Red Line runs from 5am to 1.15am Monday to Thursday (to 2.15am Friday and Saturday) and from 8am until 1.15am on Sunday.

○ Up to two pieces of luggage are permitted.

○ A travel pass called 'Nol card' must be purchased at the station.

○ Taxis wait outside each arrivals terminal 24/7. A surcharge of Dhs25 applies to rides originating at the airport, plus Dhs1.96 per kilometre.

○ Approximate taxi fares are Dhs50 to Deira, Dhs60 to Bur Dubai, Dhs70 to Downtown Dubai, Dhs110 to Madinat Jumeirah and Dhs130 to Dubai Marina.

Al Maktoum International Airport

o Dubai's new airport is a work in progress about 50km south of Downtown and receives limited flights.

o Bus F55 links the airport with the Ibn Battuta metro station hourly (45 minutes). From here, the Red Line serves most key districts.

o Taxis wait outside the passenger terminal. Approximate fares are Dhs70 to Dubai Marina, Dhs110 to Downtown Dubai and Dhs120 to Bur Dubai.

Getting Around

Metro

o Dubai metro operates two lines. The Red Line links Rashidiya near Dubai International Airport with Jebel Ali past Dubai Marina, handily parallel to Sheikh Zayed Rd. The Green Line links Etisalat with Creek station near Dubai Healthcare City.

o Trains run roughly every 10 minutes from 5am to 1.15am Monday to Thursday, to 2.15am Friday and Saturday, and from 8am to 1.15am on Sunday.

o Fares range from Dhs2 to Dhs6.50.

o For details and trip planning visit http://wojhati.rta.ae.

Taxi

o Taxis can be hailed in the street, picked up at taxi ranks or booked by phone.

o Flagfall for street taxis: Dhs8 between 6am and 10pm; Dhs9 between 10pm and 6am. Drivers accept credit cards.

o The per kilometre fare is Dhs1.82, with a minimum fare of Dhs12.

o Destinations are generally not given via a street address but by mentioning the nearest landmark (eg a hotel, mall, roundabout, major building).

Boat

o Abras (traditional wooden boats; Dh1) are a wonderful way to cross the Creek between Bur Dubai and Deira.

o Water buses (Dh3 to Dh5 per trip) are air-conditioned and link four

Nol Cards

o Travel on public transport requires the purchase of a Nol ticket or card at ticket stations or from vending machines before boarding.

o Cards must be tapped onto the card reader upon entering and exiting at which point the correct fare will be deducted.

o Short-term visitors should get the Nol Red Ticket, which costs Dh2 plus credit for at least one trip, and can be recharged up to 10 times; may only be used on a single mode of transport at a time.

o If you intend to make more than 10 trips, get the prepaid Nol Silver Card (Dhs25, including Dhs19 credit).

o For full details, see www.nol.ae.

stops around the Dubai Marina.

○ Dubai Ferry (Dh50; www.dubai-ferry.com) operates between Dubai Marina and Bur Dubai and along the Dubai Canal. Both routes interlink at Dubai Canal station.

Bus

○ Buses are clean, comfortable, air-conditioned and cheap, but they're slow and commuter geared.

○ Fares range from Dhs3 to Dhs8.50 and Nol Cards must be used.

○ For information, check http://dubai-buses.com; for trip planning, go to http://wojhati.rta.ae.

Essential Information

Accessible Travel

○ Most buildings are wheelchair-accessible, but drop-down curbs are still rare and practically non-existent in Bur Dubai and Deira.

○ Dubai's metro has lifts and grooved guidance paths in stations and wheelchair spaces in each train compartment.

○ International chains and all top-end hotels have rooms with extra-wide doors and adapted bathrooms.

○ Shopping malls are accessible, as are most bars and restaurants.

○ Some beaches, including Kite Beach and Sunset Beach, have boardwalks leading through the sand to the waterfront.

Electricity

Type G
230V/50Hz

Business Hours

○ UAE shifted its weekend from Friday and Saturday to Saturday and Sunday in 2022.

Restaurants noon-3pm and 7.30pm-midnight.

Shopping malls 10am-10pm Sunday to Wednesday, 10am-midnight Thursday to Saturday.

Souqs 9am-1pm and 4pm-9pm Saturday to Thursday, 4pm-9pm Friday.

Money

○ The UAE dirham (Dh) is pegged to the US dollar. One dirham is divided into 100 fils.

○ ATMs are widely available. Credit cards are accepted in most hotels, restaurants and shops.

○ Exchange offices tend to offer better rates than banks. Reliable outlets include UAE Exchange or Al Rostamani, both with multiple branches in shopping malls and around town.

Tipping

○ Tip porters and room cleaners Dhs5 to Dhs10 per day.

○ Waiters and spa staff get 10% to 15% of the bill (in cash).

○ In taxis round up to the nearest note.

Public Holidays

New Year's Day 1 January

Commemoration Day 30 November

National Day 2 December

Eid al Fitr Three-day celebration marks the end of Ramadan.

Eid al Adha Four-day celebration following the hajj, the main pilgrimage to Mecca.

Islamic New Year (Hejira)

Ramadan The month when Muslims fast during daylight hours.

Prophet's Birthday (Mawlid) One-day holiday for the public sector.

Safe Travel

o For the latest COVID-19-related entry requirements and possible on-the-ground restrictions, consult www.u.ae or check with the UAE embassy in your country.

o Using illegal drugs in Dubai is considered a crime and simply a bad, bad idea.

o There's a zero-tolerance policy on drinking and driving (0% is the blood alcohol limit).

o The import of certain prescription medicines is restricted unless you can present an original prescription and a letter from your doctor confirming that you need to take it. See https://u.ae/en for an overview.

o If you have an accident, even a small one, you must call the police (☎999) and wait at the scene. If it's a minor accident, move your car to the side of the road. You cannot file an insurance claim without a police report.

o Dubai is a safe city for women and it's fine to take cabs and walk around on your own.

Modest dress is recommended but there's no need to cover up.

o The Gulf may look innocuous, but rip currents can be very strong and drownings occur regularly.

Toilets

o Public toilets in shopping centres, museums, restaurants and hotels are Western style, free and generally clean and well maintained.

o The hose next to the toilet is used for rinsing (left hand only if you want to go native); toilet paper is used for drying only and should be thrown in the bin to avoid clogging the toilets.

Tourist Information

The **Department of Economy and Tourism** (☎call centre 600 555 559; www.visitdubai.com; ☉call centre 8am-8pm Sat-Thu) has no brick-and-mortar office but does maintain a comprehensive website and a call centre for information on hotels, attractions, shopping and other topics.

Islamic Holidays

Islamic Year	Ramadan	Eid al Fitr	Eid al Adha
1444 (2023)	22 Mar	20 Apr	28 Jun
1445 (2024)	10 Mar	8 Apr	16 Jun
1446 (2025)	28 Feb	29 Mar	6 Jun

Visas

o Citizens of over 50
countries are eligible for
free entry visas valid for
either 30 days (eg UK,
USA, Australia, Ireland)
or 90 days (all EU coun-
tries except Ireland) on
arrival in Dubai.

o Travellers not eligible
for an on-arrival visa
(including transit visi-
tors) must have a visitor
visa arranged through a
sponsor, such as a Dubai
hotel, a tour operator
or a relative or friend in
Dubai before arriving.

o Entry requirements to
the UAE are in constant
flux. Always obtain the
latest requirements from
www.u.ae.

Responsible Travel

Although hardly known
as a sustainable desti-
nation, there are ways
you can reduce your
impact when travelling
in the UAE.

Leaving a Lighter Footprint

o Tap water is safe to
drink in Dubai – refill

Money-Saving Tips

o Most museums and galleries are either free
or charge just a few dirham for admission.

o Top attractions such as the Dubai Fountains,
the souqs and the Creek waterfront are free.

o Take advantage of deals on drinks and nibbles during happy hours and ladies' nights.

o Travel on the Dubai metro for longer distanc-
es and use a taxi to get to your final destination
from the nearest station.

o Fuel up for pocket change on curries, kebabs,
shwarma, samosas, dosas, momos and other
exotic and delicious delectables brought to
Dubai by its global expats.

o Check out top thoroughbreds or gangly
dromedaries at highly popular horse and camel
races – admission is free.

o If you can stand the heat, visit in July or
August when hotel prices plummet.

your bottle wherever
possible.

o Frequent local cafes
and restaurants using
organic, sustainable and
regional ingredients and
offering plant-based
options. Choose wisely
at buffets.

o Use public transport
whenever possible.

o Make use of bike and
e-scooter schemes to
get around neighbour-
hoods.

o When renting a car,
make it a hybrid or
electric vehicle.

Overtourism

o Travel off-season which,
in the case of Dubai
and Abu Dhabi, means
roughly from April to Oc-
tober, with the scorching
summer months being
the least busy.

o Expand your sightsee-
ing to seek out historic
neighbourhoods, offbeat
museums, bustling
souqs and eat streets.

o Tear yourself away
from your resort and
the malls and head to
the desert to commune
with nature and the oc-
casional camel.

Language

MSA (Modern Standard Arabic) – the official lingua franca of the Arab world – and the everyday spoken version are quite different. The Arabic variety spoken in Dubai (and provided in this chapter) is known as Gulf Arabic.

Note that *gh* is a throaty sound (like the French 'r'), *r* is rolled, *dh* is pronounced as the 'th' in 'that', *th* as in 'thin', *ch* as in 'cheat' and *kh* as the 'ch' in the Scottish *loch*. The apostrophe (') indicates the glottal stop (like the pause in the middle of 'uh-oh'). Bearing these points in mind and reading our pronunciation guides as if they were English, you'll be understood. The stressed syllables are indicated with italics. The markers (m) and (f) indicate masculine and feminine word forms respectively.

To enhance your trip with a phrasebook, visit **lonelyplanet.com**.

Basics

Hello.
اهلا و سهلا.   *ah·lan was ah·lan*

Goodbye.
مع السلامة.   *ma'sa·laa·ma*

Yes./No.
نعم./لا.   *na·am/la*

Please.
من فضلك.   *min fad·lak* (m)
من فضلك.   *min fad·lik* (f)

Thank you.
شكران.   *shuk·ran*

Excuse me.
اسمح لي.   *is·mah lee* (m)
اسمحي لي.   *is·mah·ee lee* (f)

Sorry.
مع الأسف.   *ma'al·as·af*

Do you speak English?
تتكلم/تتكلمي   *tit·kal·am/tit·ka·la·mee*
انجليزية؟   *in·glee·zee·ya* (m/f)

I don't understand.
مو فاهم.   *moo faa·him*

Eating & Drinking

I'd like (the) ..., please.
عطني/عطيني   *a·ti·nee/'a·tee·nee*
الـ ... من فضلك.   *il ... min fad·lak* (m/f)

bill	قائمة	*kaa·'i·ma*
drink list	قائم	*kaa·'i·mat*
	المشروبات	*il·mash·roo·baat*
menu	الطعام	*kaa·'i·mat*
	قائمة	*i·ta·'aam*
that dish	الطبق	*i·tab·ak*
	هاذاك	*haa·dhaa·ka*

What would you recommend?
اش تنصح؟   *aash tan·sah* (m)
اش تنصحي؟   *aash tan·sa·hee* (f)

Do you have vegetarian food?
عندك طعم   *'an·dak ta·'am*
نباتي؟   *na·baa·tee*

Shopping

I'm looking for ...
مدور على ...   *moo·daw·ir 'a·la ...* (m)
مدورة على ...   *moo·daw·i·ra 'a·la ...* (f)

Can I look at it?
ممكن اشوف؟   *mum·kin a·shoof*

How much is it? بكم؟ *bi·kam*

That's too expensive.
غالي جدا. *ghaa·lee jid·an*

What's your lowest price?
اش السعر الاخر؟ *aash i·si'r il·aa·khir*

Do you have any others?
عندك اخرين؟ *'and·ak ukh·reen* (m)
عندك اخرين؟ *'and·ik ukh·reen* (f)

Emergencies

Help!
مساعد! *moo·saa·'id* (m)
مساعدة! *moo·saa·'id·a* (f)

Call a doctor!
تصل/تصلي *ti·sil/ti·si·lee*
على طبيب! *'a·la ta·beeb* (m/f)

Call the police!
تصل/تصلي *ti·sil/ti·si·lee*
على الشرطة! *'a·la i·shur·ta* (m/f)

I'm lost.
انا ضعت. *a·na duht*

I'm sick.
انا مريض. *a·na ma·reed* (m)
انا مريضة. *a·na ma·ree·da* (f)

Where are the toilets?
وين المرحاض؟ *wayn il·mir·haad*

Time & Numbers

What time is it?/At what time?
الساعة كم؟ *i·saa·a' kam*

It's/At (two) o'clock.
الساعة (ثنتين). *i·saa·a' (thin·tayn)*

yesterday ...	البارح ...	*il·baa·rih ...*
tomorrow ...	باكر ...	*baa·chir ...*
morning	صباح	*sa·baah*
afternoon	بعد الظهر	*ba'd a·thuhr*
evening	مساء	*mi·saa*

1	١	واحد	*waa·hid*
2	٢	اثنين	*ith·nayn*
3	٣	ثلاثة	*tha·laa·tha*
4	٤	اربع	*ar·ba'*
5	٥	خمسة	*kham·sa*
6	٦	ستة	*si·ta*
7	٧	سبعة	*sa·ba'*
8	٨	ثمانية	*tha·maan·ya*
9	٩	تسعة	*tis·a'*
10	١٠	عشرة	*'ash·ar·a*
100	١٠٠	مية	*mee·ya*
1000	١٠٠٠	الف	*alf*

Transport & Directions

Where's the ...?
من وين ...؟ *min wayn ...*

What's the address?
ما العنوان؟ *ma il·'un·waan*

Can you show me (on the map)?
لو سمحت *law sa·maht*
وريني *wa·ree·nee*
(علخريطة)؟ *('al·kha·ree·ta)*

How far is it?
كم بعيد؟ *kam ba·'eed*

Please take me to (this address).
من فضلك خذني *min fad·lak khudh·nee*
(علعنوان هاذا). *('al·'un·waan haa·dha)*

Please stop here.
لو سمحت *law sa·maht*
وقف هنا. *wa·gif hi·na*

What time's the bus?
الساعة كم *a·saa·a' kam*
الباص؟ *il·baas*

What station/ stop is this?
ما هي *maa hee·ya*
المحطة هاذي؟ *il·ma·ha·ta haa·dhee*

Behind the Scenes

Send Us Your Feedback

We love to hear from travellers – your comments help make our books better. We read every word, and we guarantee that your feedback goes straight to the authors. Visit **lonelyplanet.com/contact** to submit your updates and suggestions.

Note: We may edit, reproduce and incorporate your comments in Lonely Planet products such as guidebooks, websites and digital products, so let us know if you are happy to have your name acknowledged. For a copy of our privacy policy visit **lonelyplanet.com/legal**.

Andrea's Thanks

Heartfelt thanks to all the wonderful people who so graciously and generously supplied me with insider tips, background info and insights to make my Dubai research fun and fruitful, including: Rashi, Abhi and Mia Sen, Arva Ahmed, Regine Schneider, Patricia Liebscher, Christian Sanger, Dara Toulch, Janeen Mansour, Paul Matthews, Dominic Ritzer, Sameer Dasouqi, Julia Alvaro and Katie Roberts.

Acknowledgements

Cover photographs: (front) Ceiling of the Persia Court, Ibn Battuta Mall (p139), PhotoLohi/Shutterstock ©; (back) Dried herbs, flowers and spices in the Spice Souq (p38), Deira, Zhukov Oleg/Shutterstock ©

Photographs pp26–7 (clockwise from bottom left): S-F/Shutterstock ©; bennymarty/Getty Images ©; Anastasios71/Shutterstock ©

This Book

This 6th edition of Lonely Planet's *Pocket Dubai* guidebook was researched and written by Andrea Schulte-Peevers and Josephine Quintero. The previous edition was written by Andrea and Kevin Raub. This guidebook was produced by the following:

Senior Product Editor
Kate Chapman

Product Editor
Katie Connolly

Cartographer
Hunor Csutoros

Book Designer
Hannah Blackie

Assisting Editors
Imogen Bannister, Andrea Dobbin, Lauren Keith, Jodie Martire, Kate Morgan, Gabrielle Stefanos

Cover Researcher
Katherine Marsh

Thanks to Ronan Abayawickrema, Karen Henderson, Sonia Kapoor, Amy Lysen, Gary Quinn

Index

See also separate subindexes for:

⊗ **Eating p158**

☺ **Drinking p158**

✪ **Entertainment p159**

🔒 **Shopping p159**

Our Writers

Andrea Schulte-Peevers

Born and raised in Germany and educated in London and at UCLA, Andrea has travelled the distance to the moon and back in her visits to some 75 countries. She has earned her living as a professional travel writer for over two decades and authored or contributed to nearly 100 Lonely Planet titles as well as to newspapers, magazines and websites around the world. She also works as a travel consultant, translator and editor. She makes her home in Berlin. Follow Andrea on Twitter @ASchultePeevers.

Josephine Quintero

Josephine first got her taste of not-so-serious travel when she slung a guitar on her back and travelled in Europe in the early '70s. In the mid '70s she moved to the US and launched her journalism career with a wine-and-lifestyle magazine in the Napa Valley. This was followed by a move to Kuwait, where she edited the Kuwait Oil Company magazine for six years or until 1 August 1990, to be exact – the day Iraq invaded. After six weeks as a hostage and a hairy convoy escape route (via Iraq!) to Turkey, Josephine moved to the relaxed shores of Andalucía where she initially earned a crust as a ghostwriter.

Josephine primarily covers Spain and Italy for Lonely Planet. Other titles include *Mexico City, Australia, Portugal* and *Mediterranean Europe*.

Published by Lonely Planet Global Limited
CRN 554153
6th edition – Oct 2022
ISBN 978 1 78701 621 7
© Lonely Planet 2022   Photographs © as indicated 2022
10 9 8 7 6 5 4 3 2 1
Printed in Singapore